TREASURES

Short on time? - Don't miss these

GW00500783

HALL OF STEEL

Ground Floor

Pages 12 – 13

WAR

Floors 2 & 3

Pages 14 – 33

TOURNAMENT

Floors 2 & 3

Pages 34 – 45

ORIENTAL

Floors 4 & 5

Pages 46 – 59

HUNTING

Floors 4 & 5

Pages 60 – 69

SELF DEFENCE

Floors 4 & 5

Pages 70 – 80

❶ Lyle bacinet

North Italian, late 14th century. IV.470

War Gallery, Floor 2

This is one of the finest surviving examples of the 'hounskull' or 'pig-faced' bacinet. It is called 'pig-faced' because of the protruding snout.

This type of helmet has a one-piece skull, a mail aventail protecting the neck, and a removeable visor. The bacinet was the helmet most widely used by men-at-arms on the battlefield in the late 14th and early 15th centuries.

The helmet, from the Trapp family armoury at Churburg in the Italian Tirol, was a bequest of Sir Archibald Lyle, in memory of his sons Captain I A de H Lyle, Black Watch, killed at El Alamein, October 1942, and Major R A Lyle, 79th (Scottish Horse) Medium Regiment, Royal Artillery, killed in Normandy, June 1944.

French knights wearing similar helmets, from the War Gallery film of the battle of Agincourt.

❷ Warwick shaffron

Probably English, about 1400. VI.446

War Gallery, Floor 2

This shaffron (head defence for a horse) is the earliest surviving piece of medieval European horse armour. Its huge size does not mean it was for an enormous horse – inside there is evidence of rivets that would have held a thick quilted lining.

It was worn to protect a horse's head against injury. In a charge the horse's head was the first part of the animal into combat and therefore vulnerable to injury.

It was considered unchivalrous for a knight to harm the horse of an opponent during battle because a horse was considered a valuable trophy meant to be captured not destroyed.

However, in battle, warhorses were susceptible to injury from archers' arrows. Protection was initially made of cloth, then mail and later plate, mirroring the development of protection for men.

This shaffron is known as the Warwick shaffron because it was preserved at Warwick Castle from at least the 17th century. It was one of a number of objects, including a 'giant porridge pot', that were supposed to have belonged to Guy of Warwick.

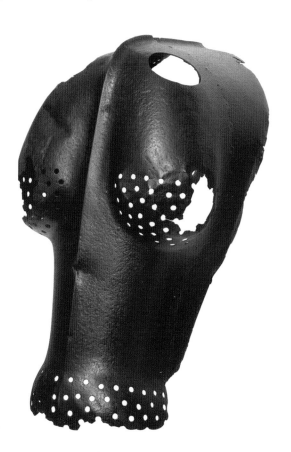

The cuts and dents on the shaffron shows that it was used in combat. There is a small square hole on the central ridge, probably caused by a bodkin-headed arrow. ▶

❸ Gothic armour

German, late 15th century.
II.3, III.69, 70, 1216, 1300, IV.15, VI.366, 379

War Gallery, Floor 2

'Gothic' armours, fashionable in Germany in the late 15th century, are usually regarded as the pinnacle of the medieval armourer's art. Slender and elegant, with attractive fluted decoration and cusped and scalloped edges, they represent the armourer's version of contemporary Gothic architecture, hence the collector's term 'Gothic' by which they are known today.

Most, like this example, are 'composite', that is, put together from disparate pieces of armour to make a complete armour from a group of pieces mounted together.

The horse armour of this example, however, is one of only five original medieval German examples in existence, a thing of great rarity indeed. The armour was probably made for Waldemar VI, Prince of Anhalt-Köthen (1450–1508).

Gothic art
Gothic is the name given to a style of European art, architecture and design in use from the late 12th to the 16th century. Today it is most easily seen in church architecture and identifiable through the use of pointed arches.

❹ Horned helmet

Austrian, Innsbruck, 1511–14. IV.22

Tournament Gallery, Floor 2

King Henry VIII's first foreign enterprise as monarch was an alliance with the Holy Roman Emperor Maximilian I (1459-1519) against the French, which culminated in victory at the battle of the Spurs (named after the speed of the French knights in retreat) on 16 August 1513.

To celebrate this alliance a magnificent armour was commissioned by Maximilian I as a gift for the young King Henry VIII. All that remains of this armour is this extraordinary helmet, made between 1511–14 by Konrad Seusenhofer, the Master Craftsman of the Emperor's imperial armour workshop at Innsbruck.

Henry would have worn the armour for court pageants rather than combat. He must have been very impressed with the Seusenhofer armour as he set up his own armour workshop in Greenwich and recruited master craftsmen from Europe to make armours for himself and favoured courtiers.

The decoration on the helmet is etched. The facial details are very life-like even down to the stubble on the chin, the crow's feet around the eyes and the drip beneath the nose.

It is currently thought that the ram's horns were added during the working life of the helmet, whose overall form represents a 'fool', an in-joke between Henry and Maximilian.

👁 Decorating armour page 45

Today the helmet is known as 'Max' and it is the motif of the Royal Armouries in Leeds – keep a look out for him on your visit and on your way home!

❺ Field and tilt armour of Robert Dudley, Earl of Leicester

English, Greenwich, about 1575. II.81

Tournament Gallery, Floor 2

This is an important Greenwich armour from the court of Queen Elizabeth I, made for one of her favourite courtiers, Robert Dudley, Earl of Leicester (1533–88).

The Dudley armour was made at the Royal Workshop at Greenwich under the Master Craftsman Jacob Halder. It is made of steel and decorated with recessed bands in the form of ragged staves, all etched and formerly gilt.

16th-century armour design tended to follow the fashion of civilian dress. The large tassets on the Dudley armour, for example, are styled on the voluminous breeches worn underneath.

👁 Making armour page 43
   Decorating armour page 45

Elizabeth (daughter of King Henry VIII and Anne Boleyn) and Dudley were friends from childhood and had a very special relationship. When Elizabeth became queen Robert was already married. His wife Amy died in mysterious circumstances and although Dudley was cleared of any wrongdoing Elizabeth could not marry him because of the risk of scandal.

Dudley was a skilled horseman and a great athlete. He served as Master of the Queen's Horse, a prestigious position which required spending long periods with the Queen organising her public appearances and entertainments. He was not a popular man; many disliked his arrogance and his monopoly of royal favour.

❻ Lion armour

Probably Italian or French, about 1545-50. II.89

Tournament Gallery, Floor 3

This is the finest decorated armour in the Royal Armouries' collections. It is damascened in gold and decorated with embossed lions' heads, and stands among the finest examples of embossed armour of the Renaissance. It was probably once a small garniture, with interchangeable pieces for the field and tournament; the helmet is marked with sword-cuts possibly received in the tourney.

An armour of this splendour would have been an outward symbol of its owner's great wealth, rank and taste.

It may have been made for the French King Henri II, either as Dauphin or soon after his accession in 1549. How and when it reached England is unknown, but it appears in a number of 17th-century portraits being worn by various sitters. Most famously this armour appears being worn by General George Monck, Duke of Albemarle (1608-70), in a portrait by John Michael Wright. It appears again in several portraits by Wright, which suggests that for some of its life the armour was an artist's studio prop.

Paintings and portraits can often be useful in tracing the origins and owners of armour.

👁 Decorating armour page 45

❼ Elephant armour (bargustawan-i-fil)

Indian, Mughal, about 1600. XXVIA.102, XXVIM.40

Oriental Gallery, Floor 4

Until the widespread introduction of firearms war elephants were a dominant force in Indian warfare. Many were provided with complete armours, yet this is the only near-complete surviving example in the world. Now weighing 118kg, when complete it probably weighed 159kg. It recently entered the *Guinness Book of World Records* as the largest and heaviest armour in the world.

It is made of some 8,450 iron plates joined by rows of riveted mail.

It is likely, judging from contemporary Mughal paintings, that most of the mail and plate armour was covered with fabric, leaving only the square panels on the body section exposed. These have embossed and engraved decoration of elephants, lotus flowers, birds and confronted fish, and have brass borders.

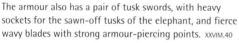

The armour also has a pair of tusk swords, with heavy sockets for the sawn-off tusks of the elephant, and fierce wavy blades with strong armour-piercing points. XXVIM.40

War elephants

Elephants played a significant part in warfare from 1000 BC until the 19th century. They were used principally in South-East Asia and India but occasionally in Western Asia, North Africa, Spain and Italy. Elephants were valued for their strength, intelligence and their ability to be trained. They were used for moving heavy loads such as forest timber and artillery pieces, but their main role was as fighting animals. They could trample men and horses alike or pick up and throw a man and horse together. They could also wield swords attached to their tusks. The reputation of elephants was so fearsome that their true military value is difficult to assess.

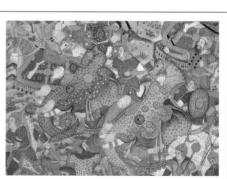

❽ Presentation sword (*jian*)

Chinese, Ming Dynasty (1368–1644), probably Yongle
period (1402–24). XXVIS.295

Oriental Gallery, Floor 4

This rare sword is one of the finest examples
of Chinese weapons as works of art in the
world. The gilded iron hilt and metal fittings of
the scabbard are covered with the finest quality
decoration. The engraving is very delicate and
intricate, especially on the pommel.

The Ming Dynasty was founded by the
Hongwu Emperor who led the revolt against
and defeated the Mongol-led Yuan Dynasty
(1279–1367). He developed a strong military
force in China because the Mongols were still
a threat to the country even though they had
been expelled.

The sword is decorated overall with Buddhist
symbols. Tibetan Buddhism became important in
China during the Mongol Yuan Dynasty and the
early years of the Ming Dynasty, and this sword
was probably made for imperial presentation to
one of the great Tibetan monasteries.

⑨ The Tula garniture

Russian, Tula, dated 1752. XII.1504, 1506, XIII.150

Hunting Gallery, Floor 4

Empress Elizabeth Petrovna.

N early all guns were made for men, but some wealthy women also owned fine guns and enjoyed shooting.

This elegantly decorated set of weapons belonged to Elizabeth Petrovna (1709–62), daughter of Peter the Great and Catherine I of Russia. In 1741 Elizabeth led a military coup and declared herself Empress of Russia. During her reign she encouraged the Russian arts, founding the Academy of Fine Arts in St Petersburg and the University of Moscow.

The garniture was made by now unknown craftsmen employed at the imperial arms workshop at Tula. It is decorated in the French style of chiselled steel on a gold background.

There are several types of weapons being used in the hunting scene on the intricately decorated stock of the sporting gun.

The complete garniture comprises a sporting gun, a pair of pistols, a powder flask, a patch box and a pair of stirrups.

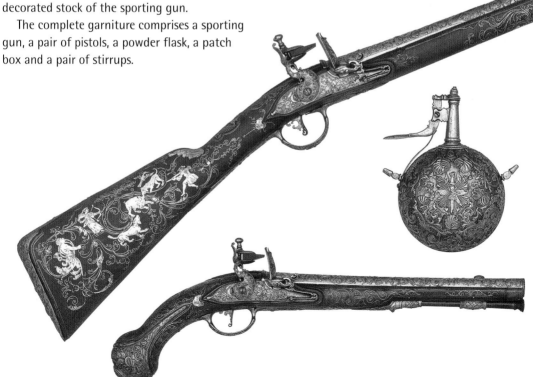

⑩ Snaphance pistol

Scottish, 1619. XII.737

Self Defence Gallery, Floor 5

This pistol is of a style in use across Britain by the end of the 16th century. It has a 'fishtail' shaped butt, octagonal breech, unguarded 'stud' trigger, and a long belt-hook. Versions with extensive Renaissance and 'Celtic' decoration became popular in lowland Scotland, and these developed into the characteristic Scottish all-steel pistol of the 18th century.

This piece has the older, more conventional wooden stock. Every available metal surface is finely engraved or pierced, and the brass is gilded. The butt decoration incorporates roses and thistles.

The snaphance lock is an early form of flintlock, and unusually is on the left side of the weapon. This shows that the pistol was originally the left-handed pistol of a pair – another particularly Scottish practice at this time.

The lockplate of this superb pistol bears the initials 'C.A.', probably for Charles Allison of Dundee. As leading gunmakers the Allison family would have supplied firearms to the Stuart royal family. This pistol was possibly made for Prince Charles, later Charles I.

Close up of lock.

Hall of Steel

The Hall of Steel is the architectural centrepiece of the Royal Armouries Museum in Leeds. This elegant steel and glass tower is unusual in that the double-glazed glass panels are fixed to an external stainless steel frame.

The displays on the stairwell consist mainly of 17th-century armour and 19th-century military equipment. There are over 2,500 items and they represent the largest mass display of arms and armour assembled since the 19th century.

The fashion for displaying arms and armour in geometrical patterns dates back to the late 17th century, when decorative displays were installed at the Tower of London, Windsor Castle and Hampton Court. The Hall of Steel display is based on those designs.

No war, or battle's sound
Was heard the world around;
The idle spear and shield
Were high uphung

John Milton

External view of the Hall of Steel.

Cannon

Bronze 18-pounder gun, French, about 1695, cast for the Duc de Beaufort. It was raised from the wreck of HMS *Association*. XIX.218

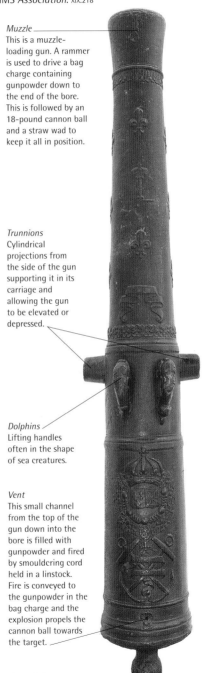

Muzzle
This is a muzzle-loading gun. A rammer is used to drive a bag charge containing gunpowder down to the end of the bore. This is followed by an 18-pound cannon ball and a straw wad to keep it all in position.

Trunnions
Cylindrical projections from the side of the gun supporting it in its carriage and allowing the gun to be elevated or depressed.

Dolphins
Lifting handles often in the shape of sea creatures.

Vent
This small channel from the top of the gun down into the bore is filled with gunpowder and fired by smouldering cord held in a linstock. Fire is conveyed to the gunpowder in the bag charge and the explosion propels the cannon ball towards the target.

Cascabel

WAR

Throughout history fighting men have tried to protect themselves from the effects of weapons in battle; at first using animal hides, leather and bone, then with the development of metalworking they used bronze, progressing to steel in the Middle Ages and now modern fabrics such as Kevlar. Body protection was adapted in response to weapons development – a momentum continued by the continual threat of conflict.

Humans have used weapons since earliest times to hunt, attack others or to defend themselves and their homes from assault by their enemies. Before the introduction of gunpowder, weapons could only be used for cutting, piercing or crushing at quite close range. With the arrival of gunpowder weapons were created that used its explosive power to fire bullets or cannon balls to longer ranges.

The displays in this gallery trace the changing face of battle from the days of bloody hand-to-hand combat to today's technology-based warfare.

The gallery displays are arranged loosely in chronological order and it is worth bearing in mind that new innovations in armour and arms did not immediately replace those that existed before. In most cases an assortment of weapons and armour were used together for long periods across these gallery time zones.

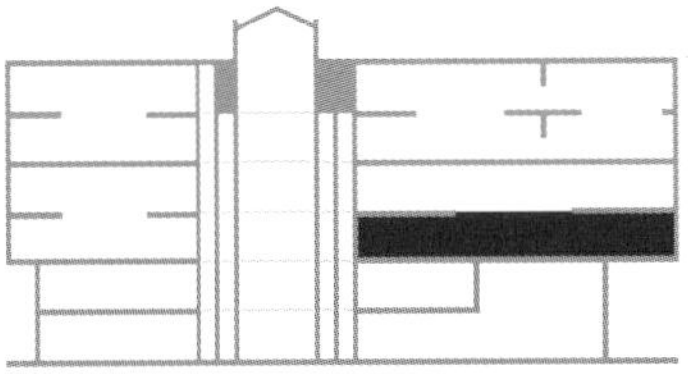

5
4
3
2
1
0

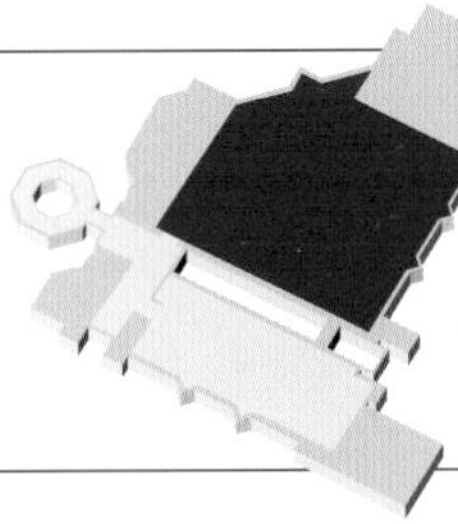

2 Warwick shaffron
👁 Treasures p3

1 Lyle bacinet
👁 Treasures p2

Battle of Pavia diorama

3 Gothic armour
👁 Treasures p4

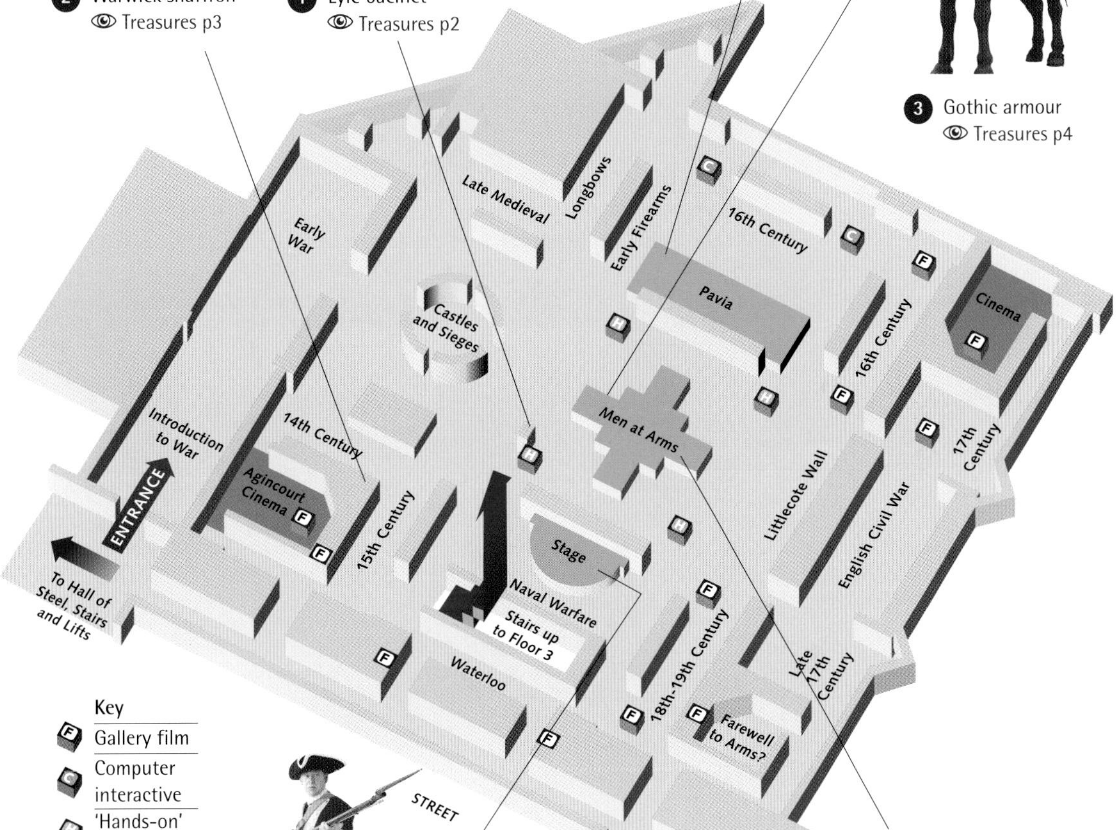

Late Medieval

Longbows

Early Firearms

16th Century

Early War

Castles and Sieges

Pavia

Cinema

Introduction to War

14th Century

Men at Arms

16th Century

16th Century

17th Century

ENTRANCE

Agincourt Cinema

15th Century

Littlecote Wall

English Civil War

To Hall of Steel, Stairs and Lifts

Stage

Naval Warfare

Stairs up to Floor 3

18th-19th Century

Late 17th Century

Waterloo

Farewell to Arms?

Key
F Gallery film
Computer interactive
'Hands-on' interactive

STREET

Bridge to Tournament Gallery

Bringing history to life!
See daily timetable for details of performances

Men at Arms display

Gatling gun

Observation Post
The Observation Post reflects the equipment used in the recent conflict in Afghanistan. Its defences show how Hesco Concertainers™ use old ideas with a new twist to protect troops against enemy fire. Firearms and kit used in combat against the Taliban are also on show, while regular handling sessions explore warfare past and present.

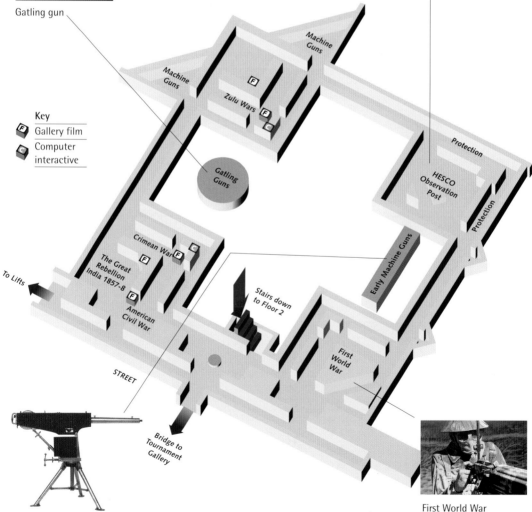

Machine Guns

Machine Guns

Zulu Wars

F

F

Key
F Gallery film
Computer interactive

Gatling Guns

Protection

HESCO Observation Post

Protection

Crimean War

F **F**

The Great Rebellion India 1857-8

F

American Civil War

To Lifts

Early Machine Guns

Stairs down to Floor 2

First World War

STREET

Bridge to Tournament Gallery

Maxim gun

First World War machine guns

Early War

The story in the War Gallery begins in the ancient world of the Greeks and Romans. Although the museum only has a few artefacts from this period, it is possible to get a good idea of the nature of ancient warfare and the arms and armour used.

▼ **Roman soldier**
Roman armies were made up of legions. A legion consisted of 5-6,000 foot-soldiers and cavalrymen, uniformly equipped and trained.

The Roman sword, *gladius*, was a short, straight two-edged thrusting sword.

The shield was a hand-held barrier to deflect blows.

Thrusting spear (*doru*)

Bronze helmet (*kranos*) and breastplate (*thorax*)

Throwing spear (*pilum*)

Blade of a Roman sword (*gladius*), 1st century AD. IX.5583

Articulated iron plates

Bronze Corinthian helmet, about 650 BC. IV.541

Iron helmet (*galea*)

Cuirass (*lorica segmentata*)

Sword (*gladius*)

Shield (*aspis* or *hoplon*)

Greave (*knemis*)

Shield (*scutum*)

▲ **Greek hoplite**
The main weapon of Greek infantry hoplites was a long thrusting spear with an iron head on a 3 metre long wooden haft.

Viking sword possibly Scandinavian, 900–1150. IX.859

Bronze armour, about 375–325 BC
This is the only complete armour from the ancient world in the Royal Armouries collection.

The armour is made up of a helmet, square breastplate, a pair of greaves, and (not shown here) a backplate, belt, pair of thigh defences and a bronze fragment from the neck defence of another helmet. Armour of this type was worn by some ranks in the legions of the Republic of Rome. II.197

Early Medieval

The period AD 400–900 is sometimes referred to as the Dark Ages. The breakdown of Roman control in Europe led to the large-scale movement of 'barbarian' peoples such as the Angles, Saxons, Norwegians and Danes. What we know about their weapons comes mostly from archaeological excavations of burial sites. Spears, shields, swords and helmets have been unearthed.

The infantry of these armies fought in dense and ordered formations. By the 10th century, the usual formation was the 'shield wall', a solid defensive line of infantry spearmen, supported by small numbers of light infantry and some cavalry - who usually dismounted for battle.

Medieval

The Medieval period, or Middle Ages, is roughly the period after the Romans left Britain until the victory of Henry Tudor at the battle of Bosworth in 1485. During the Middle Ages there were few standing armies in Britain or Europe. Men of fighting age were obliged to answer the call of their feudal lord to serve in support of the king. Many were responsible for training and equipping themselves. Paid mercenaries were also frequently employed.

Cavalry

The Normans conquered Anglo-Saxon England in the 11th century. Their military might was based on heavy cavalry charging with lances and using a sword for the second phase of close combat. Cavalrymen wore shirts and sometimes leggings of mail, a plate iron helmet and carried a kite-shaped shield.

A detail from the Bayeux Tapestry, depicting Norman cavalry charging the English shield wall at the battle of Hastings (1066). The tapestry provides some of the best pictorial evidence of arms and armour used at the time.

Mail

The High Middle Ages (11th-13th century) was the 'age of mail'. Mail was made of small iron rings riveted together. It was flexible but heavy, with the weight being carried on the shoulders. Mail was not very effective against puncturing weapons such as armour piercing arrows. Even wearing a quilted linen jacket, or gambeson, underneath could not prevent the force of a blow on mail causing bruising and broken bones. The links could be driven into the wound turning it septic.

Plate

In the 13th century, metal plates were riveted to cloth forming a 'pair of plates'. Later during the 14th century plates of iron were added to vulnerable points such as elbows and knees for extra protection and by 1400 knights were fully encased in suits of plate armour that covered most of the body.

◉ Making armour page 43

◄ **Norman cavalryman**

Mail tunic (hauberk)

Longbows

The concept of a bow made of wood, with a string of some kind of natural material and shooting a wooden arrow, is found in almost every culture on earth. Rock paintings from the Neolithic period show bows used for hunting and warfare. Archery featured in war throughout Europe before the Norman conquest of England, but gradually the longbow became especially identified with England because of a unique culture there which promoted the keeping and shooting of bows. Yeoman archers were required by law to keep bows and arrows and to practise with them every Sunday. It was illegal to play games such as football, instead of practising archery.

English archers were famous in the victories over French forces such as Agincourt, during the Hundred Years War, and later in battles like Towton (1461) during the Wars of the Roses. King Henry VIII used archers in his armies, and indeed the largest group of late medieval type English longbows which survive was recovered from Henry's flagship *Mary Rose*, which sank in 1545.

By the start of the 17th century increasingly efficient firearms, which could be used by troops with little physical strength or training, eventually brought military archery in England to an end.

Yew wood was known from prehistoric times as being the best for bow making, naturally combining a pale sapwood good at resisting stretching with a denser and darker heartwood which resisted compression. This created a superb natural spring, making very effective bows. English yew, however, grows gnarled and twisted, so yew wood for bows had to be imported from areas of Europe with a cold dry climate. To make sure that royal forces could be fully equipped with the bows they needed a form of tax was imposed by successive kings, so that lengths of yew suitable for bows would be imported into England from Europe by merchants wishing to bring in high-value cargoes such as wine.

Arrows were made of wood native to England, such as aspen (white poplar), while the fletchings were made from the flight feathers of farmyard geese, and the iron heads were forged by specialist blacksmiths.

Above: Arrowheads: left to right. A general purpose head; a military 'bodkin'; two 'broad heads' for hunting.

The other images are scenes from the films on show in the War Gallery.

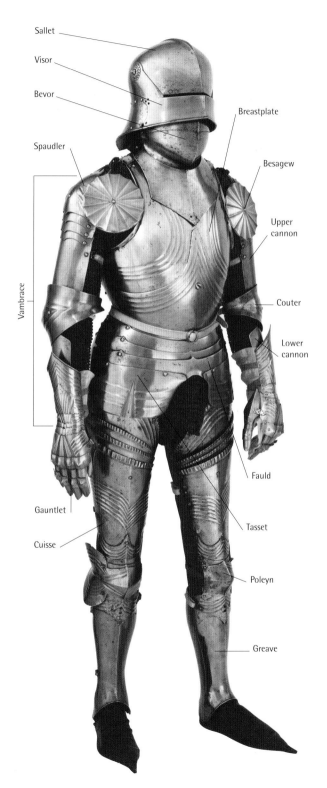

Sallet

Visor

Bevor

Breastplate

Spaudler

Besagew

Upper cannon

Vambrace

Couter

Lower cannon

Fauld

Gauntlet

Tasset

Cuisse

Poleyn

Greave

Late Medieval

From the 11th to the 15th century Englishmen fought not only in civil wars and against the Welsh and Scots but also on the Continent and in the Holy Land.

The late medieval battlefield was dominated by mounted soldiers and men-at-arms. The 14th century was the period of transition from mail to plate armour, in a response to developments in infantry weapons such as mail-piercing arrows. Shields were gradually made redundant by plate armour and disappeared from the battlefield.

Armour

By 1400 knights were almost fully encased in metal usually covered by a close-fitting coloured coat (jupon). The bottom and backs of the upper legs were unarmoured so a knight could ride his horse. By the 15th century it was fashionable to expose the bright metal of the breastplate. A full suit of armour, known as a harness, could only be afforded by wealthy knights. Most ordinary soldiers only had a simple breastplate and helmet.

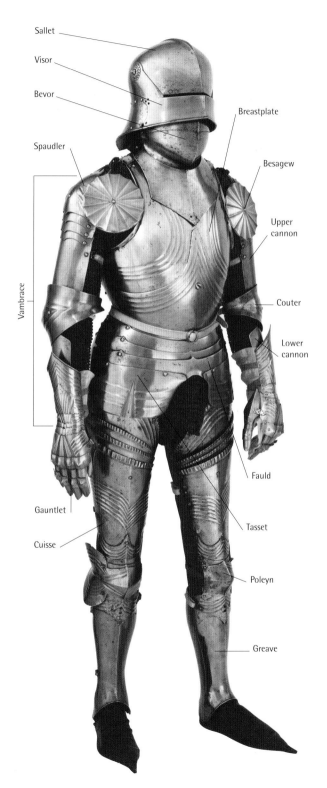 Making armour page 43

◄ **Gothic armour**
German, late 15th century.
II.1, III.853, III.1321, IV.499

16th Century

A scene from the battle of Pavia.

By the early 16th century hand-held firearms were being used in battle. They were basic, heavy to carry, slow to load, fired only short distances and were largely inaccurate.

The first battle in which infantry armed with firearms (harquebusiers) were victorious over fully armoured knights took place at Pavia in 1525 between France and the Holy Roman Empire. Metal plate armour proved no defence against bullets.

The invention of firearms did not change battle tactics overnight and for a long time a mixture of weapons was used – swords, pikes, muskets and cannon. By the later years of the 16th century European armies were using more coordinated groups of specialist troops such as musketeers and pikemen.

Armour of Sir John Smythe, about 1585. II.84

◉ Development of firearms pages 28-31

A contemporary painting of the battle of Pavia, illustrating the arms and armour of the period. I.42

Development of helmets

Head injuries are more likely than any others to be fatal and helmets have been worn in battle for thousands of years to protect the head from injury from both hand-to-hand and missile weapons. The use of traditional metal helmets declined as the use of firearms became more widespread as they provided little defence against bullets and bullet-proof helmets were very heavy. However, with the increasing use of artillery the steel helmet made a comeback in the trenches of World War I to protect against flying shell fragments (shrapnel).

1. Spangenhelm
Roman Empire – early Middle Ages
Warriors who could afford them wore a conical helmet and a mail shirt. This type of helmet was usually fitted with a nose guard. AL.102

2. Great helm
13th and 14th centuries
The great helm covered the whole head and neck. It was pierced with sights for vision and breaths for air. IV.600

3. Bacinet
14th century
An open-faced helmet with a mail aventail protecting the neck and often a pivoted visor to protect the face. IV.471

4. Armet
15th century
A helmet closely fitted to the head with hinged cheekpieces and a pivoted visor. IV.498

5. Sallet
15th century
Open-faced helmet, sometimes fitted with a pivoted visor. II.168

6. Morion
16th century
Various types of brimmed helmets without face protection were worn by infantry. IV.1565

7. Burgonet
16th century
Open-faced helmet with hinged cheekpieces. Often fitted with an articulated falling buffe. IV.569

8. Close helmet
17th century
The most favoured cavalry helmet. It opened with upper and lower bevors (chinguard) and a visor, all pivoted at the same points. IV.1026

9. Pot
17th century
Infantry and cavalry wore open-faced helmets called *pikemen's or harquebusier's* pots. IV.906

10. Shrapnel helmet
Early to mid 20th century
Helmets which could deflect shrapnel were essential during both World Wars. IV.1665

11. Ballistic helmet
Late 20th century
Combat helmets made of tough ballistic plastics. IV.1830

17th Century

The period of the English Civil Wars (1642–49) was important for changes in both arms and armour, as well as the types of soldiers employed in battle. Firearms became more important and armour was used less than before. By the end of the 17th century fixing a stout knife into the muzzle of a musket had produced the first bayonet, and gradually this development replaced the pike which had been a feature of the battlefield for over 200 years.

Foot soldiers

There were two types of infantryman employed during the English Civil Wars, the pikeman and the musketeer.

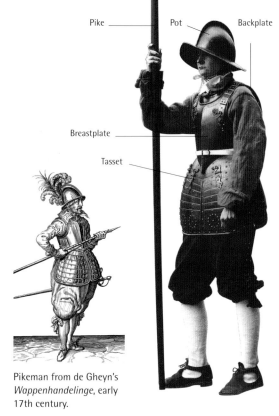

Pike — Pot — Backplate
Breastplate —
Tasset —

Pikeman from de Gheyn's *Wappenhandelinge*, early 17th century.

Matchlock musket

Bandolier

Baldrick

Sword

Musket rest

▲ Pikeman

A steel breastplate was worn over a woollen jacket. The distinctive pikeman's pot helmet was lined, but it could not stop musket balls.

◄ Musketeers

The bulk of the fighting fell to the musketeers with their relatively long-range weapons rather than to the pikeman, whose effectiveness was limited by the length of his pike. Pikemen were mainly used to protect the musketeers from cavalry charges.

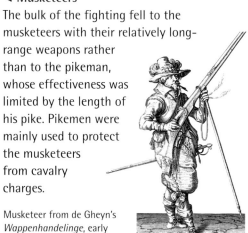

Musketeer from de Gheyn's *Wappenhandelinge*, early 17th century.

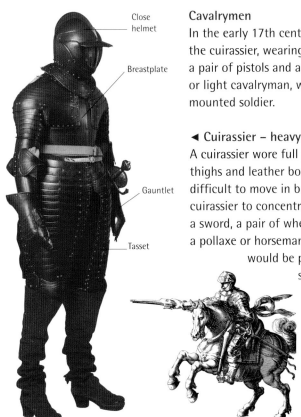

Close helmet

Breastplate

Gauntlet

Tasset

Cavalrymen

In the early 17th century the lancer had been replaced by the cuirassier, wearing three-quarter armour and armed with a pair of pistols and a sword. But the harquebusier, or light cavalryman, was the much more common kind of mounted soldier.

◄ Cuirassier – heavy cavalryman

A cuirassier wore full plate-metal armour with tassets on his thighs and leather boots. This heavy armour (20 kg) was difficult to move in but gave good protection allowing the cuirassier to concentrate on using his two pistols. He carried a sword, a pair of wheellock or flintlock pistols and sometimes a pollaxe or horseman's hammer. His breast and backplate would be proofed (tested) against pistol balls and sometimes musket balls.

Cuirassier from *Regole Militari del Cavalier Melzo*, early 17th century.

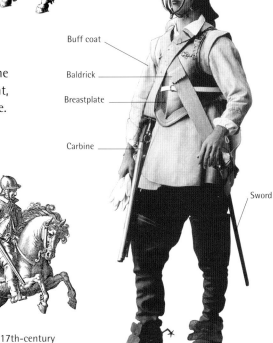

Pot

Buff coat

Baldrick

Breastplate

Carbine

Sword

► Harquebusier - light cavalryman

They wore less armour so they could handle the new style weapons; at most a leather buff coat, helmet, bullet-proof breastplate and backplate. Buff coats offered good protection against sword cuts but not pikes or guns.

They were armed with flintlock or wheellock pistols, a carbine and a sword. This meant they were able to use either firearms or charge with a sword. They were a more mobile and flexible force. Cuirassiers disappeared early in the Civil Wars, leaving the harquebusier as the only cavalry.

17th-century harquebusier.

18th and 19th Century

After the 17th century defensive armour virtually disappeared from use, in a response to the development of firearms, as it gave little protection against bullets.

Infantry armed with a musket, which could be fitted with a bayonet and used like a pike once fired, caused changes in battlefield tactics. The 18th century saw the development of 'linear' warfare, the deployment of bodies of infantry in tight formation firing in volleys and then charging with fixed bayonets. Tactics like these were employed during the American War of Independence and most dramatically in Britain's wars with France at the end of the 18th and beginning of the 19th century.

British troops advancing with fixed bayonets, from the 18th-century warfare film in the War Gallery.

Uniforms

The British Army gained its nickname the 'Redcoats' from the colour of the woollen coats the regiments wore. Oliver Cromwell's New Model Army in the 17th century was the first to wear red coats as a uniform.

The 18th and 19th century was a time of ornamental military uniforms. By mass-producing uniforms thousands of soldiers could be equipped quickly and the standard sizes and designs were easier to replace on campaign. These colourful uniforms eventually gave way in the late 19th century to khaki tunics more suited for actual combat.

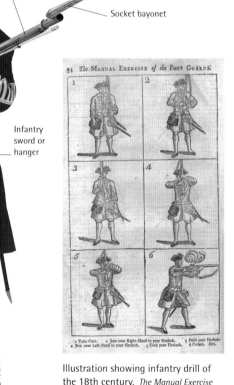

Tricorn hat

Flintlock musket

Socket bayonet

Infantry sword or hanger

18th-century British redcoat ▶
A soldier at the battle of Culloden, 1746.

Illustration showing infantry drill of the 18th century. *The Manual Exercise of the Foot Guards*

Battle of Waterloo 1815
The flintlock musket and socket bayonet of the infantry, and the sword of the cavalry were the dominant weapons at Waterloo. Large numbers of light infantry armed with rifles and French cavalry armed with lances also played a major role in the campaign.

The battle of Waterloo directed by the Duke of Wellington. Orme's Military and Naval Anecdotes, 1819.

Mass production

The early years of the 19th century heralded an industrial age the like of which had never before been witnessed.

Formerly a labour-intensive and expensive industry, by the early 1850s the production of military firearms had become largely mechanised. American manufacturers like Colt and Whitney had shown that it was feasible to use unskilled labour to produce perfectly adequate firearms, with a minimum of skilled workers for hand finishing. British entrepreneurs were not slow to adopt mechanisation and firearms manufacturers such as the London Armoury Company and the Royal Small Arms Manufactory, Enfield all used the latest technology to ensure complete interchangeability of parts, uniform fit and speed of assembly.

◉ Making firearms pages 76-7

Late 19th-century British Redcoat ▼
A private of the British 24th Regiment of Foot from the time of the Zulu Wars, 1877-79.

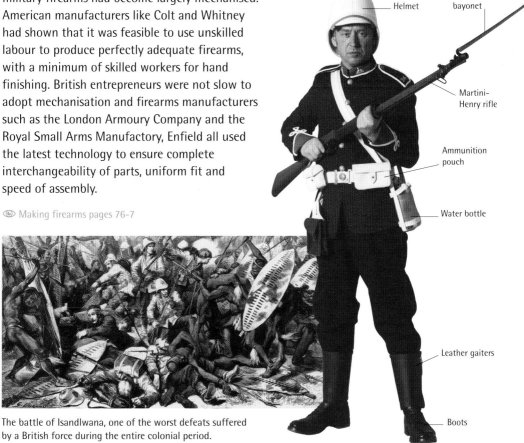

Helmet

Socket bayonet

Martini-Henry rifle

Ammunition pouch

Water bottle

Leather gaiters

Boots

The battle of Isandlwana, one of the worst defeats suffered by a British force during the entire colonial period.
Illustration by C Durand. *The Illustrated London News,* 1879

Development of firearms

What is a gun?

The first guns were simple metal tubes of cast bronze or wrought iron, closed at one end and fitted there with a touch-hole (vent). Larger guns, cannon, were placed on wooden bases to stabilize them when being fired, while smaller guns, which were light enough to be carried and fired by one person, were known as handguns. Most early guns were loaded by ramming a charge of gunpowder down to the breech (rear end of the barrel) then ramming a ball of lead down onto the powder. More gunpowder was poured into the vent and lit using a piece of matchcord (hemp cord treated with saltpetre), or with a red-hot firing iron. When the powder in the vent caught fire and ignited the main charge in the barrel the explosion of the gunpowder threw the ball out with great force.

▲ Handguns from a mid 15th-century German firework book. I.34

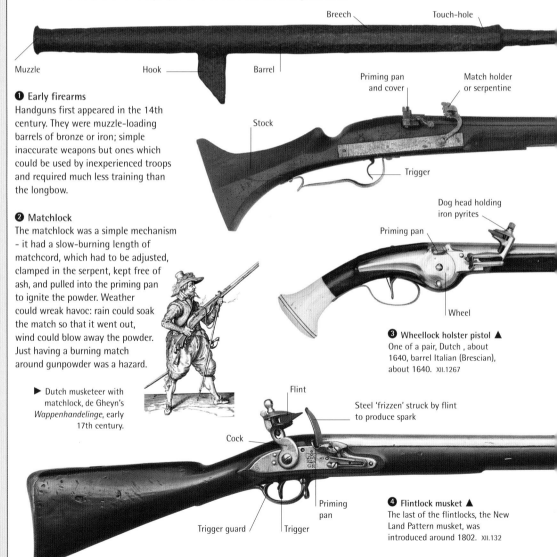

Breech

Touch-hole

Muzzle

Hook

Barrel

Priming pan and cover

Match holder or serpentine

❶ Early firearms

Handguns first appeared in the 14th century. They were muzzle-loading barrels of bronze or iron; simple inaccurate weapons but ones which could be used by inexperienced troops and required much less training than the longbow.

Stock

Trigger

❷ Matchlock

The matchlock was a simple mechanism - it had a slow-burning length of matchcord, which had to be adjusted, clamped in the serpent, kept free of ash, and pulled into the priming pan to ignite the powder. Weather could wreak havoc: rain could soak the match so that it went out, wind could blow away the powder. Just having a burning match around gunpowder was a hazard.

Dog head holding iron pyrites

Priming pan

Wheel

❸ Wheellock holster pistol ▲

One of a pair, Dutch , about 1640, barrel Italian (Brescian), about 1640. XII.1267

▶ Dutch musketeer with matchlock, de Gheyn's *Wappenhandelinge*, early 17th century.

Flint

Steel 'frizzen' struck by flint to produce spark

Cock

Priming pan

❹ Flintlock musket ▲

The last of the flintlocks, the New Land Pattern musket, was introduced around 1802. XII.132

Trigger guard

Trigger

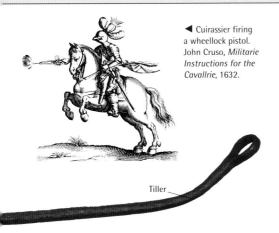

◄ Cuirassier firing a wheellock pistol. John Cruso, *Militarie Instructions for the Cavallrie*, 1632.

Tiller

❶ Early Handgun ▲
Iron, about 1500. The hook below the barrel could be placed over a wall to take the recoil. XII.3748

❸ Wheellock

By around 1500 a fire-striking device based on a tinder-lighter had been developed which used a spinning steel wheel to strike sparks from a piece of natural mineral, iron pyrites.

Having loaded the barrel with powder and ball in the usual way the lock's wheel, which was mounted on an axle driven by a strong spring, was rotated, or 'spanned' by a key about three-quarters of a turn. It was held in that position by a trigger mechanism. A piece of iron pyrites, held in a clamp or 'dog' was brought over to rest on the wheel and when the trigger was pulled the wheel spun, creating sparks which ignited the powder in the priming pan. When this powder caught fire it ignited the main charge in the barrel and fired the gun.

The wheellock enabled the creation of an entirely new weapon – the pistol. Firearms could now be used effectively with one hand and from horseback.

Barrel

❷ Matchlock musket ▲
English, about 1640. This musket is typical of those carried by musketeers of both sides during the English Civil Wars in the mid 17th century. XII.1638

❹ Flintlocks

By the 1580s a cheaper and more reliable ignition device than the wheellock had been developed which used the simple striking of flint on steel to create sparks.

A piece of natural flint was held in a spring-driven clamp, or 'cock'. A steel striking surface, or 'frizzen', was placed in front of this above a priming pan. When the trigger was pulled the cock fell forward, the flint struck the curved striking surface and threw it backwards, revealing the priming powder. Sparks fell into the priming powder, which ignited, which in turn fired the main charge in the barrel.

The flintlock went through many mechanical variations, but by the early 18th century one particular form (the French lock) became almost universal. It saw military service throughout Europe from the mid 17th to the mid 19th century.

◄ Infantry preparing to resist cavalry, with flintlocks, bayonets fixed. T L Mitchell, *Manual and Platoon Exercises*, London 1830.

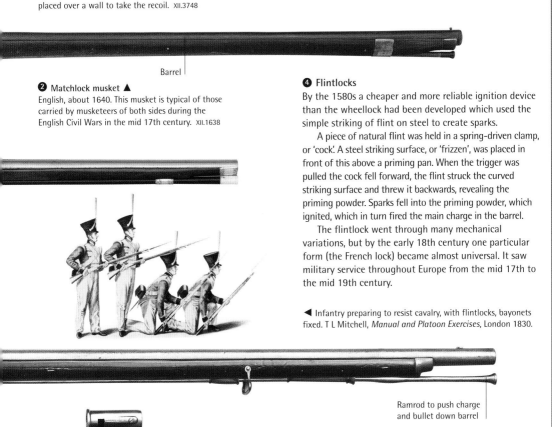

Ramrod to push charge and bullet down barrel

Bayonet

Socket to fit over muzzle

...g mass produced. At this time the ...ons, machine guns and multi-shot ...d onto the battlefield.

5 Pattern 1853 Enfield rifled musket ▼
The first rifle to be issued to all line infantry, and the first to be mass-produced, it first saw service in the Crimean War. XII.1914

Hammer   Nipple   Backsight

Falling block breech mechanism

Trigger guard / underlever

6 Sharps carbine ▲
The Sharps breech-loading mechanism, patented in 1848, was probably the most successful and widely used of all breechloaders in the percussion era. It required external ignition, achieved either by using the percussion cap or a paper strip containing pellets of fulminate. XII.2413

5 Percussion
The demise of the flintlock began in 1807 when the Reverend Alexander Forsyth experimented with fulminate of mercury. This compound detonates when struck and he experimented with it as a means of igniting the powder in a gun. This led to the development of the simpler and more effective percussion lock with its percussion cap containing fulminate and, by the 1840s, it had largely replaced the flintlock in military service.

As the cap is struck by the hammer, the fulminate explodes and sends a flame through the touch-hole to the main powder charge which fires the bullet.

Later the cap was incorporated in the base of a self-contained, metallic cartridge with the powder and ball and was loaded via the breech.

By 1840 the percussion rifle enabled the art of sniping to develop. Telescopes were soon fitted to standard military issue rifles.

6 Rifling
Flintlock and early percussion muskets were smooth-bored and, because of this, were not very accurate. For example during the battle of Salamanca in 1812, on average only one man was put out of action for every 440 musket balls fired!

Accuracy is improved by rifling – spiral grooves on the inside of the barrel make the projectile spin. For rifling to work, the grooves had to bite into the lead projectile which therefore had to fit very tightly.

Bullets
With muzzle-loading rifles, loading such a tight fitting ball was difficult and became more difficult as the bore became fouled with residues from burnt powder.

This difficulty was overcome in the 1840s by Captain Claude Etienne Minié in France. He abandoned round balls and used bullet-shaped projectiles with a hollow base. They slid into the barrel easily but at the instant of explosion, the pressure forced the sides of the hollow base outwards to grip the rifling grooves. These bullets

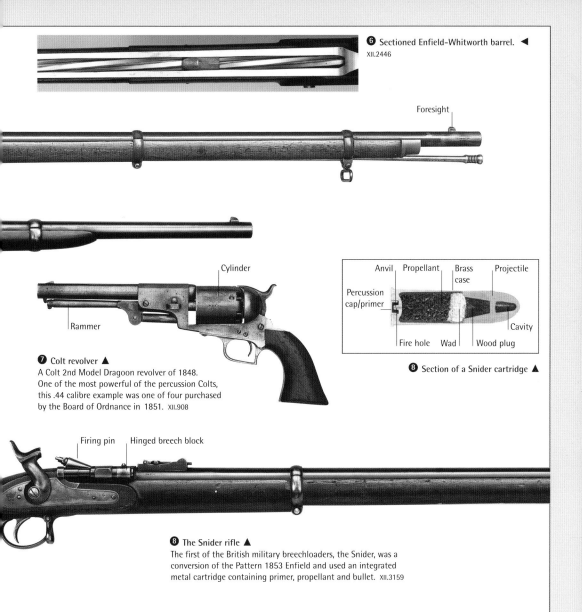

6 Sectioned Enfield-Whitworth barrel. ◄
XII.2446

Foresight

Cylinder

Rammer

7 Colt revolver ▲
A Colt 2nd Model Dragoon revolver of 1848.
One of the most powerful of the percussion Colts,
this .44 calibre example was one of four purchased
by the Board of Ordnance in 1851. XII.908

Anvil | Propellant | Brass case | Projectile

Percussion cap/primer

Fire hole | Wad | Wood plug | Cavity

8 Section of a Snider cartridge ▲

Firing pin | Hinged breech block

8 The Snider rifle ▲
The first of the British military breechloaders, the Snider, was a
conversion of the Pattern 1853 Enfield and used an integrated
metal cartridge containing primer, propellant and bullet. XII.3159

also had better stability in flight with the result that for
the first time, every soldier could be equipped with a
firearm of greater accuracy and range.

7 Revolvers
These first steps in the revolution in firearms technology
were quickly followed by others. There had always been a
desire for rapid repeat fire capability. With the percussion
system this became a more practical proposition and the
revolver, especially under the guidance of men such as
Samuel Colt and Robert Adams, was the first successful
step along this route.

8 Self-contained cartridge and breech loading
The percussion system contained the seeds of another
major advance – the self-contained cartridge and
breech-loading.
     Loading at the breech (rear end of the barrel) had
been tried before but with poor results. The greatest
drawback was having to use some form of external
ignition and also create a gas-tight seal when the breech
was closed. With the percussion cap, it became possible
to combine all the essentials of detonator, propellant
and projectile in a single unit, the cartridge, which was
self-sealing.

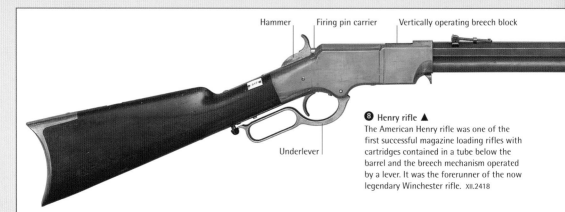

Hammer | Firing pin carrier | Vertically operating breech block

Underlever

8 Henry rifle ▲
The American Henry rifle was one of the first successful magazine loading rifles with cartridges contained in a tube below the barrel and the breech mechanism operated by a lever. It was the forerunner of the now legendary Winchester rifle. XII.2418

8 Self-contained cartridge and breech loading (*continued*)
With the development of the self-contained cartridge, it was possible to mechanise the loading and firing of guns. Magazine rifles, containing their own supply of ammunition, began to evolve in their many varied forms. The manually operated 'machine gun', in which by simply turning a handle or moving a lever backwards and forwards, the gun was repeatedly loaded and fired, began to appear.

9 Machine guns
The evolution of firearms had not yet finished. When a gun is fired it recoils - the force that sends the bullet forward also sends the gun backwards. In 1884, Hiram Maxim patented the first gun in which the cycle of loading, firing and extracting the empty cartridge case was done automatically by harnessing the energy of this recoil. This remarkable gun could fire more than 500 rounds per minute. The machine gun had been born.

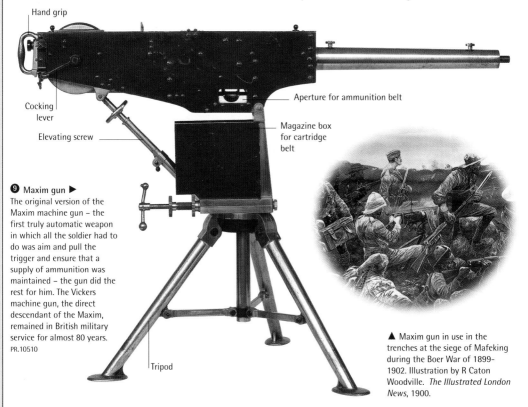

Hand grip

Cocking lever

Elevating screw

Aperture for ammunition belt

Magazine box for cartridge belt

9 Maxim gun ▶
The original version of the Maxim machine gun – the first truly automatic weapon in which all the soldier had to do was aim and pull the trigger and ensure that a supply of ammunition was maintained – the gun did the rest for him. The Vickers machine gun, the direct descendant of the Maxim, remained in British military service for almost 80 years.
PR.10510

Tripod

▲ Maxim gun in use in the trenches at the siege of Mafeking during the Boer War of 1899-1902. Illustration by R Caton Woodville. *The Illustrated London News*, 1900.

Tubular magazine

Breech block

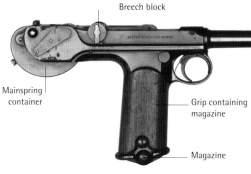

Mainspring
container

Grip containing
magazine

Magazine

⑩ Borchardt pistol ▲
The Borchardt pistol was one of many
developed in the latter years of the 19th
century. It used the energy of recoil to load
a cartridge and expel the empty case. It
required a separate pull of the trigger for
each shot fired, and is generally referred to
as an 'automatic' pistol but is more
correctly defined as 'self-loading'. The
Borchardt was the forerunner of the
famous Luger pistol. XII.3732

▶ Sailors from a
British warship use a
Gatling gun in the
streets of Alexandria,
1877. *The Illustrated
London News*, 1882.

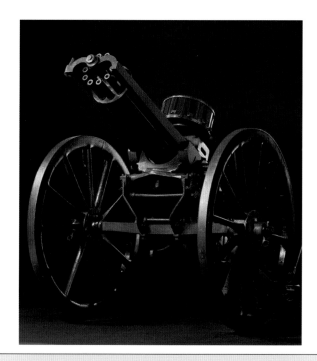

⑪ Gatling gun
The Gatling gun is often considered to be a
machine gun because it shoots a large number
of bullets in a short space of time. But unlike
modern machine guns it is not fully automatic.
A crank handle has to be operated by hand for
the gun to keep shooting.

The machine gun can be counted among
the most important technologies of the past
100 years. It set the brutal, unrelenting tone of
the First and Second World Wars. With a
machine gun a single soldier could fire
hundreds of bullets every minute, decimating
entire units. Heavy battle equipment such as
tanks had to be developed to withstand this
sort of barrage.

By the end of the 19th century, all the
fundamental concepts of firearms design and
technology had been put in place and are still
being used today.

◀ Gatling gun, 0.65 inch calibre, on naval landing
carriage. Made under licence by W G Armstrong's
Elswick Works, Newcastle-upon-Tyne, 1873. XII.1804

TOURNAMENT

Welcome to the world of tournaments. This gallery shows some of the fearsome weapons used and the special armours developed for protection in different competitions.

Tournaments were extreme sporting events that were often organised to show royal or noble power. Like modern elite sports events, many tournaments were also lavish displays that brought together competitors and spectators from far and wide.

Some tournament contests were fought on horseback, others on foot but all needed strength, skill and bravery. Over many centuries tournament events changed in both number and nature. Like football or motor racing today, rules were sometimes altered and new contests invented.

Tournament competitors needed expensive equipment, often wearing armour carefully designed to reduce risk of injury or death. Later tournament armour was also beautifully decorated. Like present-day sports kit, it combined the latest technology with style and fashion.

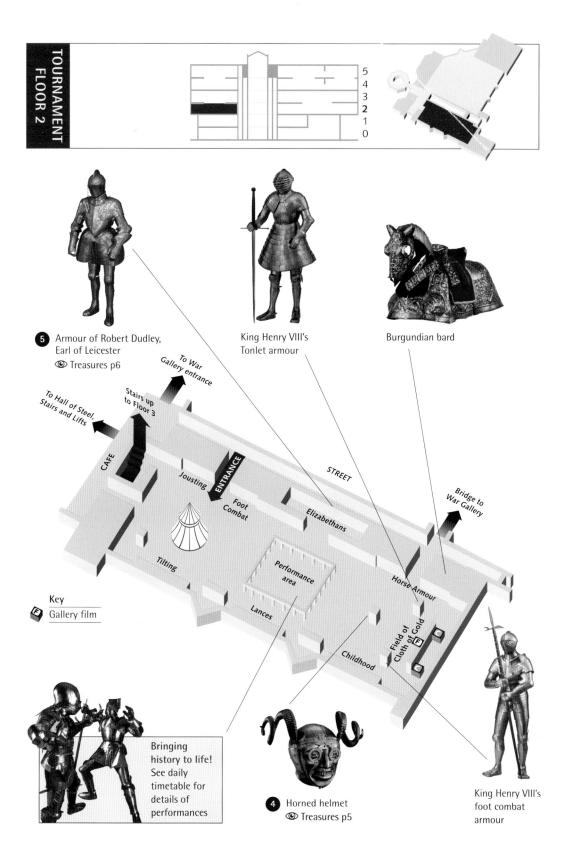

5 Armour of Robert Dudley,
Earl of Leicester
👁 Treasures p6

King Henry VIII's
Tonlet armour

Burgundian bard

To War
Gallery entrance

Stairs up
to Floor 3

To Hall of Steel,
Stairs and Lifts

CAFE

Jousting

ENTRANCE

Foot
Combat

STREET

Bridge to
War Gallery

Elizabethans

Tilting

Performance
area

Horse Armour

Key
F Gallery film

Lances

Field of
Cloth of Gold **F**

Childhood

Bringing
history to life!
See daily
timetable for
details of
performances

4 Horned helmet
👁 Treasures p5

King Henry VIII's
foot combat
armour

5
4
3
2
1
0

6 The Lion Armour
© Treasures p7

Eglinton Tournament, 1839

Stairs down
to Floor 2

To Lifts

STREET

Bridge
to War Gallery

Key
F Gallery film

Bringing history to life!
See daily timetable for details of performances
Viewing gallery for foot combat ring

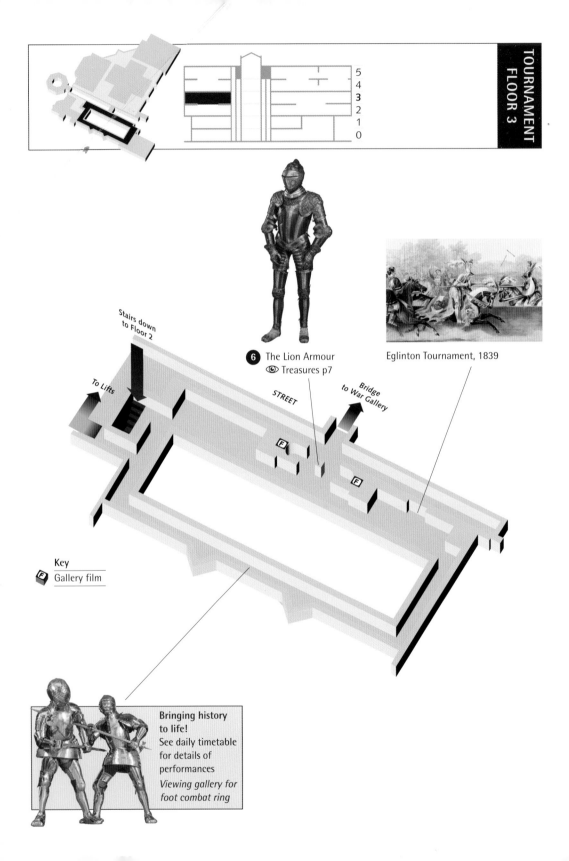

Tournament

Tournaments probably began in the 11th century as mock battles between two opposing teams and provided good training for war. Different forms of combat developed, each with its own type of armour, weapons and rules. Tournaments became spectator events, often with lavish costumes and prizes. As a colourful, chivalrous and dangerous spectacle the tournament lasted 600 years.

Types of combat

There were three forms of tournament combat – tourney, joust and foot combat. Each event had its own set of rules dictating the type of armour and weapons that could be used.

Tourney

Tourneys, especially popular in the 12th century, were fought in teams as mock battles in the countryside. Over time these events were confined to fenced enclosures. Teams fought with blunted lances and swords, wearing battle armour with many extra reinforcing pieces. The aim was to capture an opponent and hold them for ransom not to kill them, although deaths did occur in such a dangerous sport. Victorious knights were entitled to seize the

Tournament parade, from a manuscript account of the jousts between Jehan Chalons of England and 'Loys de Beul' of France at Tours, 1446.

horse and armour of those they defeated – good tournament fighters could make their fortunes this way.

Joust

The joust was a contest between two mounted knights charging at each other armed with long wooden lances. By the late 15th century there were two forms of the joust: the *joust of war*, fought with sharp, solid lances with the aim of unhorsing your opponent, and the *joust of peace*, fought with hollow lances with the aim of shattering lances.

Armour for the *joust of war*. Made for the court of the Emperor Maximilian I, about 1495. II.167

Jousting helm, Austrian, Innsbruck, about 1480, also known as the 'Brocas' helm. IV.411

The Tilt

Jousting over a barrier was called tilting, the central barrier (the tilt) was introduced to prevent collisions.

The large slot at the front of this 'frog-mouthed' helm allowed the wearer to take aim by leaning forwards. He then straightened up to protect his eyes from broken lance pieces. This meant that at the moment of impact he could see nothing and could only feel the hit!

Foot combat

Weapons used in this event included spears, maces, pollaxes or two-handed swords.

This type of combat was regulated with a set number of blows agreed beforehand and taken alternately by each knight. By the late 16th century bouts were fought over a barrier so there was no need for armour to protect the lower leg.

Heraldic Shields

In combat it was hard to identify knights wearing helmets. This meant that their bravery and skill might go unrecognised or that they might be attacked by their own side. Knights used badges so people could see who they were. These were displayed on their helmets, surcoats and shields. Some families developed coats of arms that showed who their parents, grandparents and even great-grandparents were. Many used symbols that were special to their family name or estates.

Illustration showing Ulrich von Liechtenstein with an image of Venus on his helmet. Universitätsbibliothek Heidelberg, manuscript Cod. pal. Germ. 848, f.237

The Westminster Tournament

Tournaments were often organized to mark important occasions. The more special the event, the more impressive were the celebrations. The Westminster Tournament was held on 12 and 13 February 1511 to mark the birth of a son and heir for Henry VIII.

Henry VIII is jousting over a tilt barrier, scoring points by breaking his lance into three pieces against his opponent's helm. In the stand sit King Henry's wife, Katherine of Aragon, her ladies and important guests.

The College of Arms, London

King Henry VIII

Henry came to the English throne in 1509 at the age of 18. As a young man he excelled at tennis and wrestling and enjoyed skill at arms, archery, jousting and foot combat.

Field of Cloth of Gold June 1520
The accession of François I to the throne of France brought a change to the diplomatic relations between France and England. This new friendship was embodied in the most magnificent tournament ever held, called the Field of Cloth of Gold as the kings' tents were made with cloth of gold.

The two kings met between Calais and Guines, on the border of the English enclave around Calais and French territory, and the festivities lasted for about two weeks. This extravagant and expensive event took months of planning. The tournament

Portrait of Henry VIII, after Holbein, oil on panel, English, late 16th century. I.51

culminated in the signing of a peace treaty between the two powers, as well as giving the two young kings ample opportunity to show off their chivalric skills.

King Henry who, at 29 years old and 188cm (about 6ft 1in) tall, was a fine athlete, took part in many of the combats. It is said that on one particular day he ran so many courses that his horse died of exhaustion!

The Field of Cloth of Gold, artist unknown. The Royal Collection © 2014 HM Queen Elizabeth II

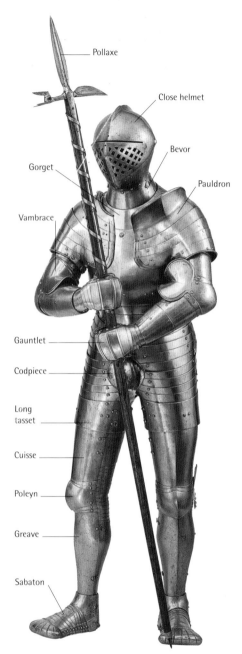

Pollaxe

Close helmet

Bevor

Gorget

Pauldron

Vambrace

Gauntlet

Codpiece

Long tasset

Cuisse

Poleyn

Greave

Sabaton

▲ Foot combat armour

This armour was in production for Henry VIII to wear at the Field of Cloth of Gold, but was never completed. A change in the rules for the armour worn in the foot combat event occurred and work on this armour ceased and it remained undecorated. II.6

▼ Tonlet armour

The armourers at Greenwich had a very short time to make a new armour for Henry VIII to wear at the Field of Cloth of Gold. They succeeded in preparing this armour, known as the Tonlet armour because of its hooped skirt of that name, by adapting a number of existing pieces, manufacturing additional pieces from new, and decorating the armour. Only the pauldrons and the tonlet were made new. II.7

Great bacinet

Two-handed sword

Pauldron

Tonlet

Horse armour

One of a knight's most valuable possessions was his best horse and because he owned a 'cheval', or horse, in French he was called a 'chevalier'. A horse needed special protection in tournaments and war.

Horse armour was introduced to protect the horse's head, neck and flanks against blows from lances, swords and, in battle, arrows. Horse armour was first made of textiles or mail. However, from about 1450 steel plate was used.

▼ The Burgundian Bard
This horse armour was a gift from the Holy Roman Emperor Maximilian I to Henry VIII to mark his marriage to Katherine of Aragon in 1509. It is described in an English inventory of 1519 as 'given by the Emperor'.

It is embossed with a trailing design of pomegranates (Katherine's badge) and the firesteels and ragged (raguly) crosses of the Burgundian Order of the Golden Fleece which Henry had been awarded in 1505. Flemish, about 1511–14. VI.6-12

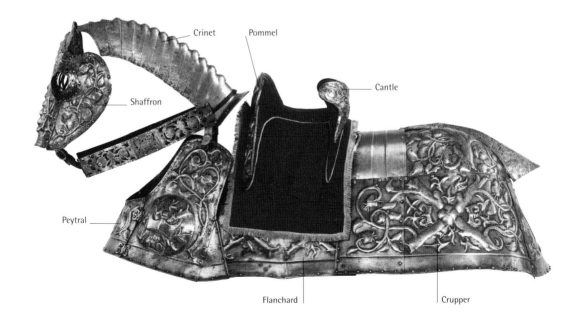

Crinet

Pommel

Cantle

Shaffron

Peytral

Flanchard

Crupper

Gloriana: Queen Elizabeth I

When Henry VIII died he was succeeded by his children – first young Edward VI, then Queen Mary and finally Queen Elizabeth I. The royal armourers at Greenwich worked solely for the monarch but Queen Elizabeth probably never wore armour, nor did she have a husband or son who needed it.

The Queen found a profitable way of running the workshop. She permitted favoured courtiers to order armours, for which they paid heavily. The Royal Armouries has the finest collection of these Elizabethan courtiers' armours. Some of the owners can be identified in the *Jacob Album* of master armourer Jacob Halder.

Sir Henry Lee
Sir Henry Lee was Elizabeth's champion in the 1580s and he arranged her Accession Day jousts in the 1590s.

Elizabeth I, c. 1588.
The Bridgeman Art Library

Tournaments
As a woman Queen Elizabeth I did not compete in tournaments. However, from1580 Elizabeth's knights held special tournaments on 17 November each year to celebrate the anniversary of her accession to the throne. These took place at Whitehall Palace and included not only tournament games but also poems, speeches and plays praising the Queen.

Elizabeth's favourite knights enjoyed the exclusive but very expensive privilege of her approval to order armour from her Greenwich royal armoury. Some spent so much on tournaments and armour to stay in favour that they sank deep into debt.

▼ Armet for the tilt of Sir Henry Lee
This helmet was made in the royal workshop at Greenwich under the master armourer, Jacob Halder. English, Greenwich, about 1585. IV.43

Portrait Anglo-Flemish, late 16th century. I.379

Making armour

Metal

Iron ore, a rock rich in iron, is found in the earth's crust and is mined like coal. Iron is obtained by melting the iron ore at very high temperatures. Although strong and hard, this heavy grey metal rusts easily.

Steel is formed by melting iron ore and mixing it with carbon in a blast furnace. Steel is harder and tougher than iron and does not rust as easily.

Mail

Mail was made up of small, linked riveted iron rings. It was a skilled and time consuming art. A mail coat weighed about 9-14 kg (20-31 lb). Mail coats worn with iron helmets were gradually replaced by plate armour in a response to weapons development.

A mail maker's workshop.

Plate armour

Plate armour needed to fit its wearer well if it was to work effectively and not be unbearably uncomfortable, but having an armour made to fit was expensive, and could really only be afforded by wealthy individuals. The overall shape of armour often followed trends in civilian fashion. Some royal and noble owners also displayed their wealth by having the appearance of their armours enhanced with costly etched and gilded decoration.

For the tournament special armours could be made, or those intended for use in battle could have additional pieces to provide extra protection when being used for example when jousting. Some mobility could be sacrificed and extra weight made acceptable if the armour was only to be used in a particular way and for a short period.

Munition armour was provided to troops in military service and was not made to fit a particular individual. It did, however, provide useful protection, and was made to a form for particular types of soldiers, whether infantry or cavalry, or for others such as sappers and miners. Elite guards could even have decoration on their armour, by which their unit might be recognised.

Fabrication

The raw materials of the armourer's craft were steel plates. Hot sheets of metal were beaten out by heavy hammers at a battering mill. The armourer, using templates, would cut the shapes needed to make the armour out of these sheets of steel using shears. The piece would then be hammered into the rough shape of the particular part of the armour. The heated metal was then shaped on small anvils or specially shaped stakes; ball-shaped stakes were used for helmets and cylindrical stakes for leg and arm pieces.

Polishing

After shaping, the armour would look discoloured by fire and dimpled by the hammer blows. The parts now had to be smoothed and polished. This was done on a mill using graded grit stone. The last milling was done with a leather-coated buffing wheel and emery powder for a fine finish. This work was usually done by a specialist millman.

The armour was now ready for decorating. The embellishment was done in a separate specialist workplace away from the dust of the armourer's workshop.

Dressing to impress

When armour was custom-made for a particular client his measurements would be taken and the armourer would work from flexible card patterns. The decoration could be customised or chosen from a pattern book. Major artists such as Dürer and Holbein were involved in designing armour decoration.

Inside armour

The inside of the armour might be painted to protect it from rusting caused by condensation from sweat and breath. Padded linings were sewn inside after the decorating process. Hinges, buckles and leather straps were made by a locksmith. Sliding rivets eased the movement of joints.

Emperor Maximilian I in the workshop of his court armourer, Konrad Seusenhofer. *Der Weisskönig*, early 16th century.

Centres of excellence

The finest armour and weapons were produced in Southern Germany and Northern Italy. Towns such as Milan, Augsburg and Nuremberg were renowned for their master armourers. The wealthy imported armours from abroad, as England had no comparable talent. This particularly galled Henry VIII who could not reciprocate in kind when he was presented with high quality armours by European monarchs. So he set up his own armour workshop in Greenwich staffed by foreign craftsmen, referred to as 'Almayns' (Germans) in contemporary documents. To have an armour made at Greenwich required a royal licence.

Fashion

16th-century armour tended to follow the forms of civilian dress. Puffed and slashed costume of the early 16th century was copied in armour. A shorter, rounder breastplate developed a central ridge and a longer waist like the Elizabethan doublet (see the Dudley armour below). Longer tassets reflected the voluminous breeches worn underneath. In the 17th century breastplates became shorter and flatter and the tassets covered from the waist to knee. (See cuirassier page 23).

Garniture

All the different sets of armour that a competitor needed to compete in all the tournament events and the vast expense of having armour made led to the development in the early 16th century of the 'armour garniture'. A complete armour, which would usually be designed for the 'field' (battlefield) was provided with the additional pieces necessary for it to be converted into a tilt, foot combat or tournament armour (see below).

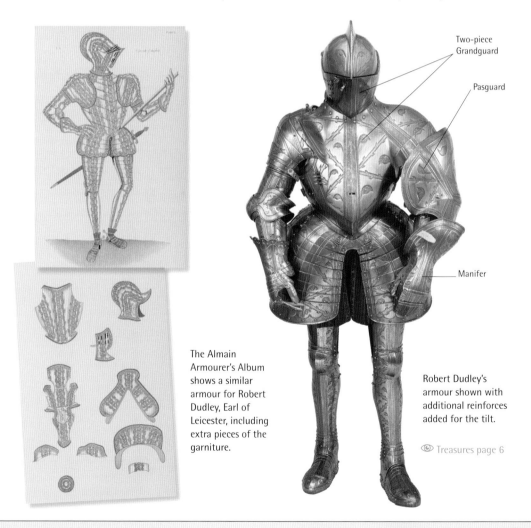

Two-piece Grandguard

Pasguard

Manifer

The Almain Armourer's Album shows a similar armour for Robert Dudley, Earl of Leicester, including extra pieces of the garniture.

Robert Dudley's armour shown with additional reinforces added for the tilt.

Treasures page 6

Decorating armour

Decorating armour

Part of the ornamentation process involved marking a design on to the visible surface of any object. To do this meant the removal of some of the metal in a controlled manner in order to put down the design or pattern.

The two main methods are either physically cutting away the metal using tools (engraving, chasing, chiselling and punching) or by eating the metal away using acid (etching).

The quality of the design engraved or etched depended on the skill and experience of the craftsman.

Engraving

The main technique for adorning metal was to cut away the surface of the metal using special tools – gravers, chisels, little hammers and files.

Right: Detail showing engraving on the Charles I gilt armour.

Chasing

Chasing is used to work on the front of the metal by pushing the metal down. The opposite of chasing is repoussé (pushed up) in which the metal is shaped from the reverse. The two processes were used together to create a finished piece. This slow process uses the plasticity of the metal, creating the design by degrees.

Etching

Etching was a common form of decoration on armour. Etch comes from the Dutch and German words meaning to eat or corrode. The design is eaten into the surface of the metal using a corrosive acid.

The etcher's pattern was often selected from illustrated book of patterns intended as models for use by craftsmen and makers of decorative objects.

The whole surface of the metal was painted with protective wax or varnish. A master drawing was made of the chosen design which was then pricked through the paper onto the metal using a series of dots, scratching through the resist (wax or varnish) and exposing the metal underneath.

Then the surface was treated with acid. The acid ate into the metal where the wax had been cut away. Afterwards the wax was washed away with a solvent such as turpentine. The etched design was emphasised by rubbing it with lamp-black in oil.

Alternatively the design could be preserved by the protective wax and the background etched away, using small dots or cross-hatching, leaving the design in slight relief.

Detail showing etching and gilding on the Smythe armour.

Gilding and silvering

The ancient art of gilding is the process of applying a thin layer of gold or silver to a surface. The process usually involved applying an amalgam of the precious metal and mercury to a part of the armour and heating it. The mercury evaporated and the gold and silver became firmly attached to the metal.

Damascening

This is the art of cutting a narrow groove into the steel, hammering gold or silver wire into these recesses and then polishing the whole surface.

Right: Detail showing damascening and embossing on the Lion armour.

Blueing

The armour needed to be polished to a mirror finish. The iron was heated in a kiln or oven. It was a skill to control the heat and make sure the whole piece developed an even colour. The finished colours ranged from peacock blue through to black.

Detail showing blueing on the Elector Christian I armour.

ORIENTAL

Arms and armour have been made and used around the world for war, sport, military practice and self-defence.

This gallery concentrates upon the great civilisations of Asia, and its purpose is to show how arms and armour can provide a key to understanding Asian history.

The cultures of Asia are far more diverse than those of Europe, and the gallery is divided into a number of distinct zones – Central Asia, Turkey, Persia, Islam, the Indian sub-continent, China, Japan and South East Asia. There is one theme that unites all these diverse cultures and has dominated the way in which war was waged in most of them until the 19th century: the use of the mounted archer.

5
4
3
2
1
0

Mounted samurai warrior

8 Presentation sword
👁 Treasures p9

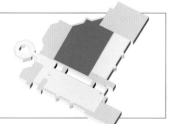

Bringing history to life!
See daily timetable for details of performances

Mongol horseman

To Hall of Steel,
Stairs and Lifts

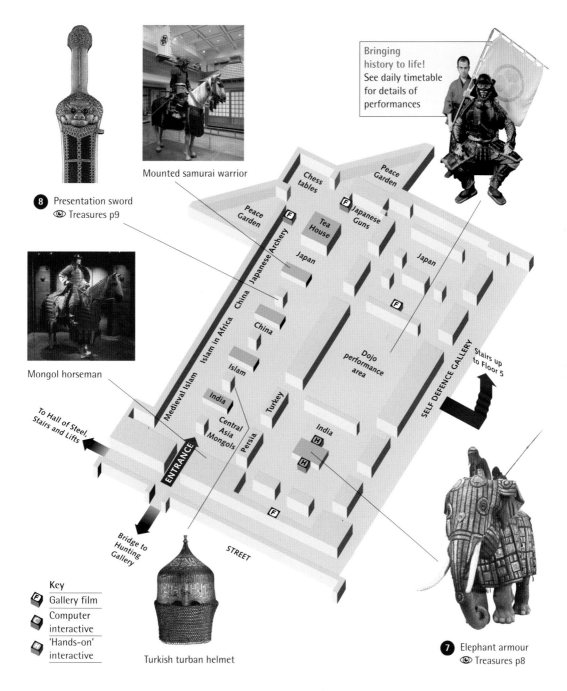

Chess tables

Peace Garden

Peace Garden

F Japanese Guns

Tea House

Japanese Archery

Japan

Japan

China

F

China

Dojo performance area

Islam in Africa

Medieval Islam

Islam

India

Turkey

SELF DEFENCE GALLERY

Stairs up to Floor 5

Central Asia Mongols

Persia

India

H

H

ENTRANCE

F

Bridge to Hunting Gallery

STREET

Key
F Gallery film
◆ Computer interactive
◆ 'Hands-on' interactive

Turkish turban helmet

7 Elephant armour
👁 Treasures p8

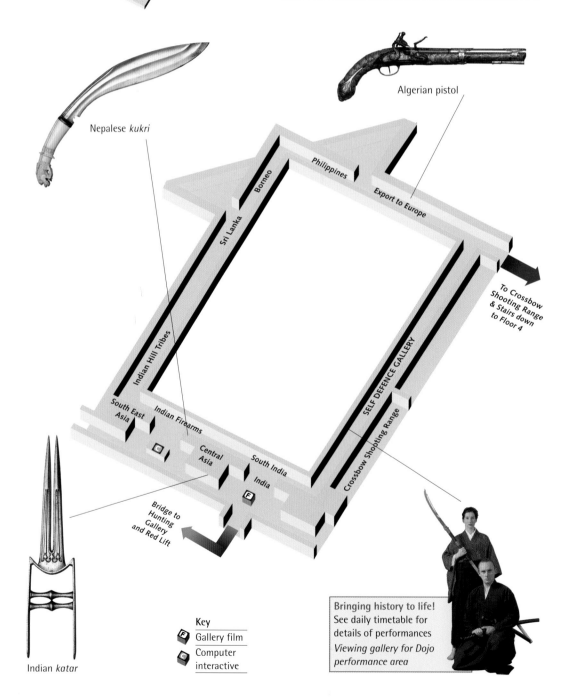

5
4
3
2
1
0

Nepalese *kukri*

Algerian pistol

Philippines

Borneo

Sri Lanka

Export to Europe

To Crossbow
Shooting Range
& Stairs down
to Floor 4

Indian Hill Tribes

SELF DEFENCE GALLERY

South East
Asia

Indian Firearms

Central
Asia

South India

India

Crossbow Shooting Range

Bridge to
Hunting
Gallery
and Red Lift

F

Indian *katar*

Key

F Gallery film

Computer
interactive

Bringing history to life!
See daily timetable for
details of performances
*Viewing gallery for Dojo
performance area*

Islam

The rise of Islam

The rise of Islam both as a religion and a world
power was an extraordinary phenomenon.
The Hijri era, still used throughout the Islamic
world, began with the Hijra (flight or
migration) of the Prophet Muhammad from
Mecca to Medina in AD 622. Victory at the
battle of Badr (AD 624) established
Muhammad's ascendancy over western Arabia,
and by the time of his death in AD 632 his
authority was supreme in most of Arabia.

Turks and Mongols

The Turkish military system, based on the use of
armoured horse archers, was introduced into
the Islamic world in the 9th century. They came
first as slave soldiers (*ghilman*), but by the
11th century founded their own Muslim
dynasties and empires. The central Asian
Mongolian tribes, who fought in the same way,
conquered most of the established Islamic
dynasties in the west under Genghis Khan in
the 13th century and China in the east under
Kubilai Khan. With the break-up of the great
Khanate, however, most of the Mongol
successor states also embraced Islam. The most
powerful Islamic empire in the west by the
15th century was the Ottoman Turkish empire;
the Ottomans captured Constantinople in 1453
using heavy artillery, and built an empire that
controlled northern Africa, western Asia and
eastern Europe until the mid-19th century.

▼ Mongol heavy cavalryman

This equipment was used from the wars of
conquest in the 13th century to the 17th
century when lamellar armour was replaced by
mail and plate armour. The principal weapon
was the composite bow, but many were armed
with a lance and sword as well.

Armour and equipment of a Mongol cavalryman,
15th-17th century, helmet later. Horse armour lent by Victoria
& Albert Museum. XXVIA.122, 157, 276, XXVIB.141, 145, XXVIH.21, 22, 38A,
38B, AL.189.18, 189.21

Turkish sword (*kılıç*),
about 1560. XXVIS.293

China

Many military inventions came from China, including the crossbow and perhaps most important of all, gunpowder. Chinese arms and armour could also be great works of art.

◄ Lamellar armour

This is typical of the leather lamellar armours of western China. Lamellae are small plates of rawhide, heavily lacquered to protect them from the effects of moisture, the lacing being leather. Some scales are decorated with carving. These may have formed decorative borders to the armour, or may have been incorporated from an earlier coat, when the armour was last re-laced. The helmet is constructed of laced plates and bordered with leopard skin. Similar lamellae have been excavated from 6th-century sites in Chinese Central Asia, demonstrating the long period of use of this form of armour.

Lamellar armour from Sichuan, probably 18th century. XXVIA.106

◄ Armour

During the early Ming dynasty (1368–1644), these so-called 'brigandine' armours became the commonest type in China. They consist of a jacket of heavy fabric with separate sleeves, all covered with embroidered silk and lined with numerous, small tinned iron plates fastened by gilt rivets. To this were added ornately shaped shoulder guards, leg defences and originally an iron helmet with a plate-lined fabric neck guard.

Ding jia armour, probably 17th century. XXVIA.135–6

India

Arms and armour feature as a central part of Indian culture from earliest times. The heroes of early epic stories such as the *Mahabharata* ride on chariots and shoot bows, and archery plays a central role in all Indian military systems until the widespread introduction of firearms in the 18th century.

> **The Mughals (Moguls)**
> A Muslim dynasty of Mongol origin, ruled most of India between the 16th and 18th centuries (regnal dates).
> 1527–30 Babur (descended from Genghis Khan)
> 1530–56 Humayun
> 1556–1605 Akbar the Great
> 1605–27 Jahangir
> 1627–58 Shah Jahan (builder of the Taj Mahal)
> 1658 –1707 Aurangzeb

Armour

The earliest forms of armour from India are of scale.

Mail and plate armour was probably introduced into India under the Mughals. Coats and helmets were made from small overlapping iron scales connected by rows of mail links. Coats had large plates at the front and quilted linings. Trousers of mail were worn on the legs.

In the late 18th century this type of armour was replaced by four plates joined by straps. This was copied from contemporary Persian armour.

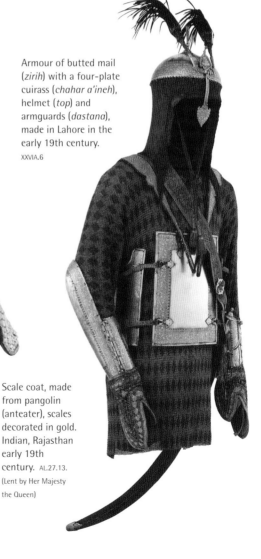

Armour of butted mail (*zirih*) with a four-plate cuirass (*chahar a'ineh*), helmet (*top*) and armguards (*dastana*), made in Lahore in the early 19th century.
XXVIA.6

Scale coat, made from pangolin (anteater), scales decorated in gold. Indian, Rajasthan early 19th century. AL.27.13. (Lent by Her Majesty the Queen)

Mail and plate horse armour (*bargustawan*). Mughal, about 1600. XXVIH.18

Horse armour

The provision of horse armour was very important in warfare where the bow was the most important weapon on the battlefield, and the horse the most common target. Horse armour ceased to be used in the late 17th century, probably because of the increased effectiveness of firearms on the battlefield.

Archery

The composite bow was the characteristic missile weapon of both Indian cavalry and infantry before the 18th century.

Shields

Most medieval and later shields are circular, slightly convex, fitted with two hand hoops riveted through the shield and secured with large bosses on the exterior. The interior was often lined in fabric.

War elephants

Treasures page 8

Swords

With the introduction of central Asian cavalry warfare into India from the 13th century onward, the Asian curved blade sword became the preferred type throughout much of India. The indigenous Indian sword had a straight double-edged blade, and this survived into the post-medieval period as the *khanda*. From the early 17th century there was a fashion for carrying swords with European rapier or broadsword blades (*firanghi*).

Dagger (*khanjar*), Mughal, late 17th century. XXVID.145

Curved sword (*talwar*), 17th century. AL.290 60
(Lent by Her Majesty the Queen)

Sword (*firanghi*), 18th century. XXVIS.83

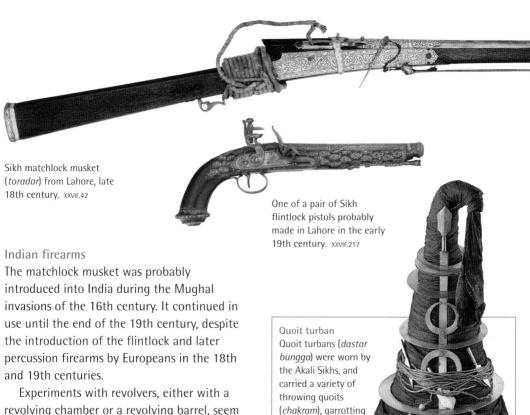

Sikh matchlock musket (*toradar*) from Lahore, late 18th century. XXVIF.42

One of a pair of Sikh flintlock pistols probably made in Lahore in the early 19th century. XXVIF.217

Indian firearms

The matchlock musket was probably introduced into India during the Mughal invasions of the 16th century. It continued in use until the end of the 19th century, despite the introduction of the flintlock and later percussion firearms by Europeans in the 18th and 19th centuries.

Experiments with revolvers, either with a revolving chamber or a revolving barrel, seem to have started quite early in India. Samuel Colt studied examples of these at the Tower of London during his development of the revolver in the middle years of the 19th century.

Quoit turban
Quoit turbans (*dastar bungga*) were worn by the Akali Sikhs, and carried a variety of throwing quoits (*chakram*), garrotting wires and knives.

Quoit turban, Lahore 18th century. XXVIA.60

Arms of south India

During the late 18th century, the latest military technology was deployed in the Sultanate of Mysore, but in the rest of south India the arms and armour were very conservative. The medieval Indian straight and flamboyant swords continued to be used until the 20th century and a number of peculiar weapon forms survived.

Tipu Sultan of Mysore

Tipu Sultan was ruler of the southern Indian state of Mysore from 1782–99. An ally of France, he was killed at the siege of Seringapatam fighting against the British forces of the East India Company.

Fabric armour (*peti*) and helmet of Tipu Sultan, Mysore, late 18th century. XXVIA.139

Japan

Much of Japan's early culture was imported via Korea from the great civilisation of Tang dynasty China (AD 608–907). Chinese characters, which are the basis of Japanese writing, and a great deal of the social structure were imported. All the armour and weaponry associated with the medieval samurai have their origins on mainland Asia at this time.

Detail showing the early stages in putting on an *o-yoroi* (lamellar armour). From an early 19th-century copy of *The order of arming of Minamoto Yoshiiye*

Samurai

The ancient Japanese warrior class is known as the *bushi* or samurai. The samurai had rights and privileges, but also obligations – including the requirement to fight for and give complete loyalty to his feudal master. From 1192, when Minamoto Yoritomo was named Shogun, to the restoration of the Meiji Emperor to political power in 1868, the samurai class effectively ruled Japan. The lesser samurai owed allegiance to their feudal lords or *daimyo* ('great names') who formed the land-holding aristocracy.

▶ **Samurai warrior** Wearing a replica of a 16th-century *tosei gusoku* armour.

Helmet (*kabuto*)

Turnback on neckguard (*fukigayeshi*)

Neckguard (*shikoro*)

Face mask (*mempo*)

Shoulder guards (*sode*)

Body armour (*do*)

Armoured sleeve (*kote*)

Hip and thigh defence (*gessan*)

Thigh defence (*haidate*)

Shinguards (*suneate*)

Equipment of a samurai of the Edo period. Armour probably 18th century, equestrian equipment modern.
XXVIH.42, XXVIA.42, AL.268 5

Yabusame

Yabusame is the art of shooting arrows from a galloping horse at a series of stationary targets situated along a straight track. The sport is closely related to the ancient horse archery games of mainland Asia.

The current practice of yabusame is almost exclusively considered a religious rite: as well as being an offering to the gods, the results of the shooting at the three targets are used in some centres as a divination ritual for the year's harvest.

The broken fragments of the cedar targets are considered lucky, and are signed and dated and distributed after the event as souvenirs.

'Armour of the Great Mogul'

The arms and armour of Japan are very important in the collections of the Royal Armouries. The very first Asian armour to enter the collection was this Japanese armour – one of the armours presented in 1613 to King James I by Shogun Tokugawa Hidetada, son of Shogun Tokugawa Ieyasu.

This armour is displayed at the Tower of London, where it has been on show since at least 1660, when it was known as the 'armour of the Great Mogul'. The armour was restored and relaced in 1972. The helmet is an *akoda nari kabuto* with its typical gilt decoration on the bowl. It was made by Iwai Yozaemon of Nara.
XXVIA.1

The Japanese sword

The Japanese sword is unique in the world in its cultural status. It is one of the divine objects of the Shinto religion, incorporating air, earth, fire and water in its production.

A contemporary Japanese swordsmith in his forge.

It acquired a shape and method of construction around AD 1000 that later swordsmiths were unable to improve upon. The long sword became a symbol of rank for the military class, the *buke*. Famous artists were employed to design the sword's furniture (fittings) and the most skilled craftsmen to translate these designs into metal.

Historical swords and armours are much more highly regarded in Japan than elsewhere because of the Shinto association of these objects with the spirits of the dead.

▼ Short sword (*wakizashi*) by the swordsmith Tadahiro of Hizen Province, mid 17th century, with fittings and accoutrements of the later Edo period. XXVIS.198

Scabbard (*saya*)   Sword guard (*tsuba*)   Hilt (*tsuka*)

Blade   Tang (*nakago*)

Firearms

Firearms were introduced to Japan by Portuguese traders in 1543 and forward-thinking commanders began to equip their low ranking soldiers with them. As in Europe, the finest swordsmen could be defeated by a peasant armed with a gun after only a few hours training. Old-style lamellar armour was virtually useless against bullets, simple armours of plate began to appear on the battlefield.

▶ A matchlock gunner. The coil around his wrist is a supply of match that would last for a day.
Zobyo Monogatari, 1846

▼ Matchlock musket (*teppo*) by Enamiya Ihei, early 19th century. XXVIF.52

The interior of an armourer's workshop during the 16th century. From a reproduction of a 16th-century genre screen of trades

Lacquer

Lacquer is the sap of a small tree and is obtained, like rubber, by tapping the trunk and scraping off the viscous sap as it exudes. After processing, the sap forms a varnish-like liquid that hardens irreversibly when exposed to warm, moist conditions to form a hard yet flexible waterproof coating. In its natural state, hardened lacquer is a dark brown colour but for finishing coats it was generally coloured black with carbon or iron compounds, red with vermilion pigment or various shades of brown by mixing the two. Most other pigments, as used in paints, could not be employed since they reacted chemically with the lacquer.

Lamellar armour

Early Japanese armours were lamellar, that is, the major components were made up from lamellae, small scales of iron or rawhide called *sane*. The armour was elegant, efficient against arrows, spears and swords but was very delicate and easily damaged. The silk laces soaked up moisture and eventually needed replacing. The armour was also prone to become infested with lice and fleas.

During the 16th century the increase in the scale of conflict and the quantity of armour needed in the civil wars, as well as the lengthening of the campaigning season, led armourers to simplify the armour they made. Instead of forming elements from the traditional lamellae, they used solid plates, often lacquered to simulate lamellae. The lacing was simplified so it was easier to keep clean and much quicker to make. Helmets were simplified too: the multi-plate types of the Middle Ages gave way to simple three- or five-plate types. These were often decorated with elaborate crests formed of papier-mâché and lacquered.

Armour (*tosei gusoku*) laced with blue silk, made for a member of the Sakakibara family, 16th century. XXVIA.274

South and South East Asia

The hill peoples of central India

The hills and jungles, which separate the Indus–Ganges Plain in the north from the Deccan and the south of India, were a significant barrier to military and political expansion. They prevented all but the most determined invaders from conquering the south of the subcontinent. Armies that ventured into this territory were often lost for months at a time. The impenetrable terrain isolated the many scattered tribal communities from each other and from the outside world.

The arms of Sri Lanka

Sri Lanka developed distinctive weapons including the dagger (*piha kaetta*) and the sword (*kastane*).

▼ Naga sword (*dao*) with offset blade from Assam, 19th century. XXVIS.244

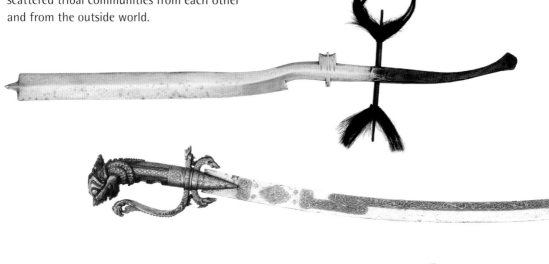

▲ Sri Lankan sword (*kastane*) blade probably 19th century, hilt early 17th century. Purchased with the aid of the Art Fund. XXVIS.167

▲ Sri Lankan dagger (*piha kaetta*) and silver-mounted scabbard, probably 18th century. XXVID.82

Malaya and Indonesia

The national weapon of Malaya and Indonesia is the *kris*. The *kris* is traditionally made of a mixture of meteoric iron and steel; the characteristic pattern, which looks like water, on the blade is produced by corroding the metal with a mixture of lime juice and arsenic. The *kris* was carried by all adult males, tucked into the back of the sarong at the waist.

The Philippines

The armour developed by the Moro people of the Philippines is unique. It is of mail and plate construction, the plates being of horn and the mail of brass, a style clearly influenced by the armour of the medieval Islamic world. The helmets were also constructed from horn and brass, but in the style of European burgonets of the 16th century, influenced by contact with early Portuguese explorers and traders.

Arms of mainland south-east Asia

In Burma the weapons used were very similar to those of the south-western Chinese peoples. The name of the sword, the *dha*, is linguistically allied to the Chinese *dao*. Crossbows were used extensively in warfare and hunting, and these show a type of lock mechanism far more primitive than those used by the Chinese in the 3rd century BC. Elephants played an important role in warfare as shock troops. Marco Polo in the 13th century described Burmese war elephants carrying as many as sixteen crewmen. Most of this region is covered in dense jungle, and infantry and elephants were most important as the terrain is not suitable for cavalry warfare. Although the Mongols conquered this area, they found it very hard going, and were unable to retain control for long.

Arms of Tibet and Nepal

The Central Asian curved sword never became fashionable in Tibet where the long single-edged sword, used until the 10th century by the steppe peoples, survived. In Nepal, on the south side of the Himalayas, very different swords were used. The earlier type is the *kora*, a forward-curved sword, almost always decorated on the wide point of its blade with an eye.

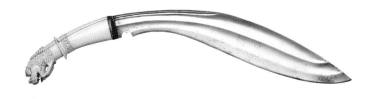

◀ A Nepalese *kukri* with an ivory hilt carved in the form of a lion, made in the 19th century. XXVID.30

◀ Tibetan sword and scabbard, 17th–19th century, with silver fittings set with turquoise and coral. XXVIS.187

HUNTING

The history of hunting is traced from prehistoric times, having its origins in the need to survive. Our distant ancestors were hunter-gatherers and probably first killed small animals to supplement a diet of wild foods such as berries, nuts, vegetables and honey and to put warm furs on their backs. They made weapons, nets, traps and tools out of natural materials such as wood, bone, ivory and stone and eventually metal.

It was only when man discovered how to grow crops and domesticate animals that he stopped living as a hunter-gatherer. Settled communities produced enough food for survival and there was now an opportunity to learn other crafts.

Even though the need to catch food to survive declined over time, man's love of hunting continued. Hunting offered excitement, tested strength, courage, skill and was an opportunity for the wealthy to show off, as can be seen by some of the fabulously decorated weapons on display in this gallery.

To many today hunting is repulsive and indefensible, to many it is right and natural, and to some it is still essential for survival. It is this story, both good and bad, which is told in this gallery. We also consider weapons as works of art, as the evidence of the pinnacle of a craftsman's skill.

5
4
3
2
1
0

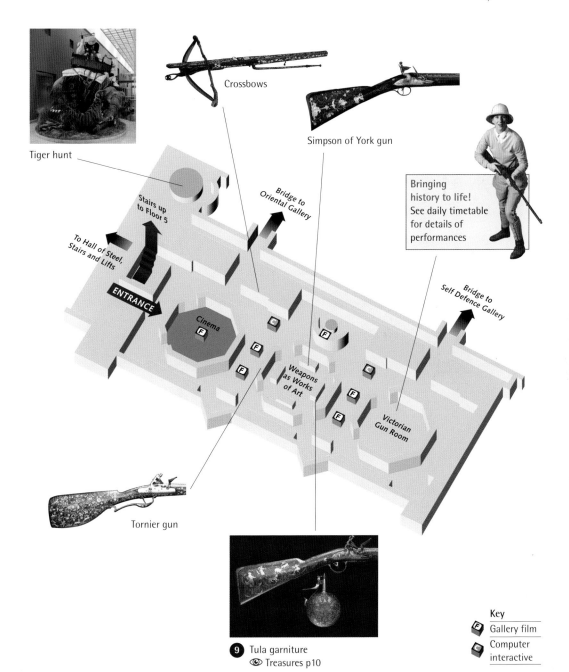

Tiger hunt

Crossbows

Simpson of York gun

Bringing
history to life!
See daily timetable
for details of
performances

Stairs up
to Floor 5

Bridge to
Oriental Gallery

To Hall of Steel,
Stairs and Lifts

ENTRANCE

Cinema

Bridge to
Self Defence Gallery

Weapons
as Works
of Art

Victorian
Gun Room

Tornier gun

9 Tula garniture
👁 Treasures p10

Key
Gallery film
Computer
interactive

5
4
3
2
1
0

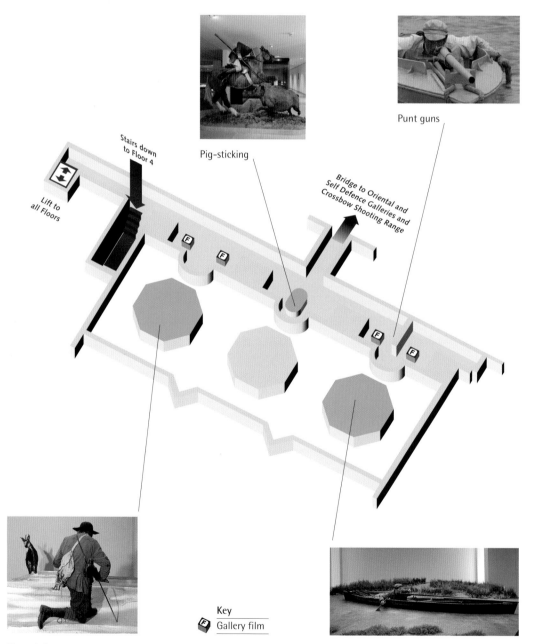

Stairs down
to Floor 4

Pig-sticking

Punt guns

Bridge to Oriental and
Self Defence Galleries and
Crossbow Shooting Range

Lift to
all Floors

F

F

F

F

Key
F Gallery film

Chamois hunt

Punt gunner

Hunting weapons

Longbows

From prehistory bows were used to hunt game, and indeed are still in use in some countries today. However in England, where the longbow was such an important weapon of the armies of the Middle Ages, its use was restricted to the noble classes. Ordinary people, who were required by law to practise in its use for war, were strictly forbidden to hunt with it.

👁 Longbows page 20

Crossbows

The longbow was a simple instrument but was only deadly in the hands of a skilled archer. By comparison a crossbow was a more complicated and expensive weapon, but required little skill to use. As it was slower to use than a longbow it was more suitable for siege defences and hunting rather than on the battlefield.

Crossbows are believed to have been invented by the Chinese in the 4th century BC. It was not until the 10th or 11th centuries (AD) that the crossbow became a military weapon in Europe. With the introduction of hand-held firearms it passed out of general military [use in the] 16th century but its use for h[unting and] shooting has continued to th[is day.]

A crossbow is a projectile [weapon which,] depending on the type, shoots arrows, bolts, quarrels, stones or bullets. It consists of a bow attached crosswise to a stock called a tiller. Whereas a longbow is used vertically the crossbow is used horizontally. The tiller is fitted with a trigger mechanism for the release of the bowstring. Early crossbows were spanned by hand but as technological developments made stronger bows possible they became more difficult to span this way and mechanisms were invented to overcome this. The result was that projectiles could be shot with greater force.

Smaller animals and birds were frequently shot at with bows made to shoot balls of fired clay or lead, since their bodies were easily penetrated by arrows which might not actually stop them escaping the hunter. The shock effect of a blunt arrow or a ball was likely to kill small creatures more effectively.

While the longbow remained plain and unadorned throughout its life, highly decorated crossbows became quite common by the 15th century.

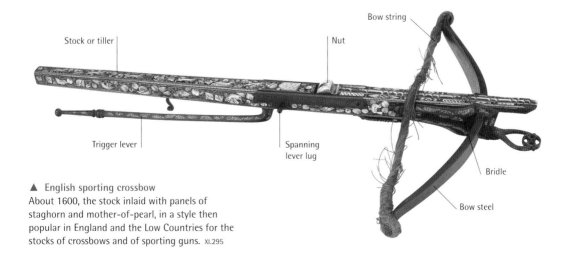

Stock or tiller | Nut | Bow string

Trigger lever | Spanning lever lug | Bridle | Bow steel

▲ English sporting crossbow
About 1600, the stock inlaid with panels of staghorn and mother-of-pearl, in a style then popular in England and the Low Countries for the stocks of crossbows and of sporting guns. XI.295

Firearms

Firearms appeared in Europe in the early 14th century, but there is little evidence that they immediately began to replace the existing projectile weapons then in use. The inaccuracy of these early guns, and the noise and smoke they produced, would have made them less successful than bows or crossbows as hunting weapons.

Improvements in gun making gradually made them more effective, however their use in hunting, until the end of the 17th century at least, was restricted to shooting at birds while they were at rest. Shooting at flying birds

Detail from Shooting Flying, an illustration in Richard Blome's *The Gentleman's Recreation*, 1686.

required an effective ignition system, and by around 1700 flintlock guns designed to shoot birds on the wing had been developed.

The flintlock always posed a problem for the sportsman, however, in that the puff of smoke from the priming powder was often seen by the bird at which he was shooting, giving the bird a brief but sufficient opportunity to 'jink', or turn suddenly, causing the charge of small lead shot to miss its mark.

Percussion ignition, invented in the early years of the 19th century by a keen Scottish sporting clergyman, the Reverend Alexander Forsyth, provided a major breakthrough in smokeless ignition, and is still the way by which almost all modern small arms cartridges are fired today.

Airguns

Airguns of considerable power and sophistication saw some use both militarily and for hunting, since the absence of powder smoke and their almost silent operation did not disturb the intended target or indeed others around it, whether human or animal. Rechargeable reservoirs containing compressed air allowed for a number of discharges, but the complexity and cost of such weapons meant that they did not achieve the widespread use of the more powerful, and less expensive, black-powder sporting guns.

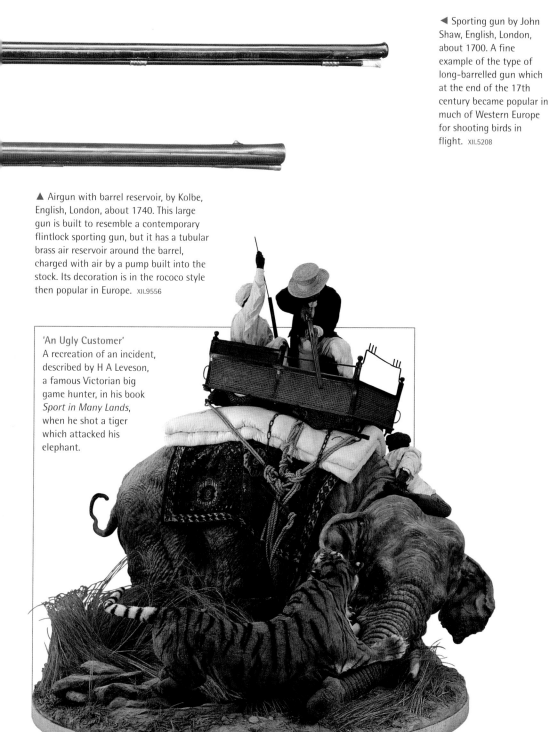

◄ Sporting gun by John Shaw, English, London, about 1700. A fine example of the type of long-barrelled gun which at the end of the 17th century became popular in much of Western Europe for shooting birds in flight. XII.5208

▲ Airgun with barrel reservoir, by Kolbe, English, London, about 1740. This large gun is built to resemble a contemporary flintlock sporting gun, but it has a tubular brass air reservoir around the barrel, charged with air by a pump built into the stock. Its decoration is in the rococo style then popular in Europe. XII.9556

'An Ugly Customer'
A recreation of an incident, described by H A Leveson, a famous Victorian big game hunter, in his book *Sport in Many Lands*, when he shot a tiger which attacked his elephant.

Punt gunning
A reconstruction of a famous Essex punt gunner, Walter Linnet, paddling his punt, using 'creeping sticks', quietly towards a flock of wildfowl. Punt gunning required great skill and stealth but one good shot could kill many birds.

▼ (left) Hunting hanger, hilt Italian about 1660, blade English, about 1730 The iron hilt is chiselled in the form of three dragons. IX.977

▼ (right) Hunting hanger, probably Dutch and made between 1650 and 1670. The cast and chased silver hilt is in the form of a lion being attacked by hounds. IX.849

Edged weapons

A number of different edged weapons were used in hunting, some depending upon which animal was the quarry. Boars and bears, for instance, which were both large and dangerous, were hunted with specially designed thrusting spears and swords. These weapons had crossbars which stopped the blade penetrating too deeply, which otherwise might not be easily withdrawn and, equally importantly, did not allow the wounded animal to slide up the blade and gore the hunter.

Once the animal had been killed the carcass would be butchered in preparation for the banquet that often followed such a grand social occasion. Some hunting swords had saw-back blades with which to dismember the kill. Special sets known as trousses included various choppers, bodkins, knives and forks, designed to be used for both the preparing and eating of the game.

Spears and swords for the chase were also very often heavily decorated, displaying both the owners' rank and wealth. Hunting hangers, for instance, which were shorter swords with a straight

The charge, a print from *Hog hunting in Lower Bengal* by Percy Carpenter, 1861.

▼ Hunting spear, French or Italian, about 1600. The lower part of the blade, the socket and the toggle are encrusted with gold and silver. VII.81

or slightly curved single-edged and pointed blade, and used for game such as deer, often had hilts made of precious materials such as ivory, cast bronze, semi-precious stone, or even porcelain. The blades themselves were often etched and gilded. Indeed some hangers are nothing less than small masterpieces of decorative art.

Falconry

Falconry is a hunting partnership between man and bird. The art is to cast the bird from your wrist into the sky from where it spies its prey, soars to its pitch and swoops down at speeds of up to 120 mph, killing the prey with a knock-out blow from its talons. It is one of the world's oldest sports and it is believed to have started in Mesopotamia over 4,000 years ago. In the Middle Ages it was a popular sport in Europe and an efficient way for catching small mammals and birds for the table. The introduction of firearms almost brought to an end the art of falconry – guns are more efficient weapons and do not need daily feeding and exercise!

Weapons as works of art

Until the 15th century weapons used for hunting were little different to those used in war, indeed a major purpose for members of the nobility of the pursuit on horseback of large game such as wild boar was to become familiar with the threat of injury or death in the face of real danger. From the 15th century onwards, however, it became more common to decorate weapons used in hunting, to demonstrate the wealth and status of their owner. This developed further later, as hunting itself became a major social and courtly pursuit.

Crossbows

Crossbows, whether intended to shoot bolts or bullets, had their steel bows decorated with etching and gilding, and their stocks were often inlaid with stag horn, mother-of-pearl and other materials.

Firearms

Firearms gradually became the predominant hunting weapons, with finely crafted shotguns for shooting birds and small game, and rifles to take larger animals. Good quality weapons were costly, and their owners were of course fashion conscious. It is no surprise, therefore, that fashion played a major part in their decoration, since any owner would wish his gun to be decorated in the latest style of the day in exactly the same way that he would wish any of his furniture or other household effects to be.

Decoration

A variety of craftspeople would have been engaged in the making of most weapons; barrel makers, lock makers and stock makers, for example, were augmented by those who specialised in different decorative techniques. The surface of metal components could have motifs applied in gold or silver by damascening or false damascening, or could have designs and inscriptions made by engraving them.

▶ Crossbow
For shooting stones or pellets. Traditionally the property of Marie Leczinska (1703-68) who married Louis XV of France in 1725. XI.93

▲ Simpson Gun
This gun was made in 1738 for William Constable of Burton Constable Hall, East Yorkshire by William Simpson, a York gunmaker. It is regarded as the finest provincially made English sporting gun of the 18th century.
　　The decoration is of the highest quality. The lock and the steel furniture of the stock are all chiselled in relief with rococo ornament. The stock is inlaid with silver wire. The designs depict angels, cherubs, and a lion and a unicorn lying together beneath a palm tree. XII.5843

Chiselling could create decorative elements in relief, which was in metal a similar technique to the carving often applied to wooden gun and crossbow stocks. Such stocks could also receive inlaid decoration using a wide variety of materials, including precious metals to horn, staghorn and mother-of-pearl.

Damascened decoration appears on the iron parts of fine guns by the early 16th century, when stocks were carved and sometimes upholstered for the comfort of their users. In the 17th century throughout much of Western Europe the form of gun components and their chiselled and engraved decoration formed part of an international style developed by a number of French artist craftsmen, who published their designs in a series of exquisitely engraved pattern books.

Design plate for gunmakers, by Claude Simonin, Paris, 1684.

Craftsmanship

Finely decorated hunting weapons continue to be made today, since owners are still keen to show that for them a weapon is not only a tool to do a job, but a vehicle for the finest craftsmanship both in construction and in decorative taste. Thus the restraint of the fine engraving found on best quality London-made shotguns still contrasts with lavishly-decorated sporting guns made for hunting enthusiasts in Europe and America.

Finely decorated hunting weapons were often given as expensive gifts, in some cases as diplomatic gifts to show respect to the recipient but also to demonstrate the power of the giver. Some of the most exquisitely decorated guns and swords can be seen in the centre of the Hunting Gallery.

👁 Decorating armour page 45

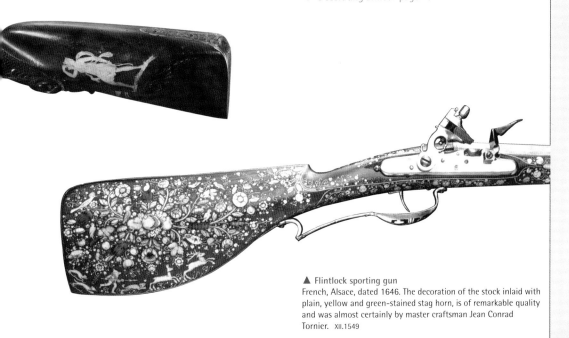

▲ Flintlock sporting gun
French, Alsace, dated 1646. The decoration of the stock inlaid with plain, yellow and green-stained stag horn, is of remarkable quality and was almost certainly by master craftsman Jean Conrad Tornier. XII.1549

SELF DEFENCE

Many objects in the Royal Armouries collection have a social relevance today - perhaps none more so than those in the Self Defence Gallery. Individuals have always suffered attacks by other members of the community, who want to harm or steal from them, and society has tried to organise itself in various ways to control these crimes of violence. For example changes to the law are once again under discussion with the aim of restricting public access to guns and knives. The Self Defence Gallery displays are occasionally updated to explore important new developments, such as gun crime in the local community.

A highly topical issue at present is what kind of protective equipment is most likely to save the lives of police officers or security guards who are attacked by violent criminals. Recent tragic events have shown that even the latest body armours have their limitations – just as the mail shirt or brigandine was no guarantee of safety centuries ago. New materials are invented and used, but the perfect armour has still not been made.

Similarly, the question of which weapons the police should carry is one that has often been debated. However, perhaps the greatest change has been the tightening of laws on which weapons ordinary citizens in the UK may legally own or use. In attempts to limit the deadly effects of conflict, whole categories of both guns and knives may no longer be legally bought or carried in public – a real contrast to a few generations ago, when many families possessed at least one firearm.

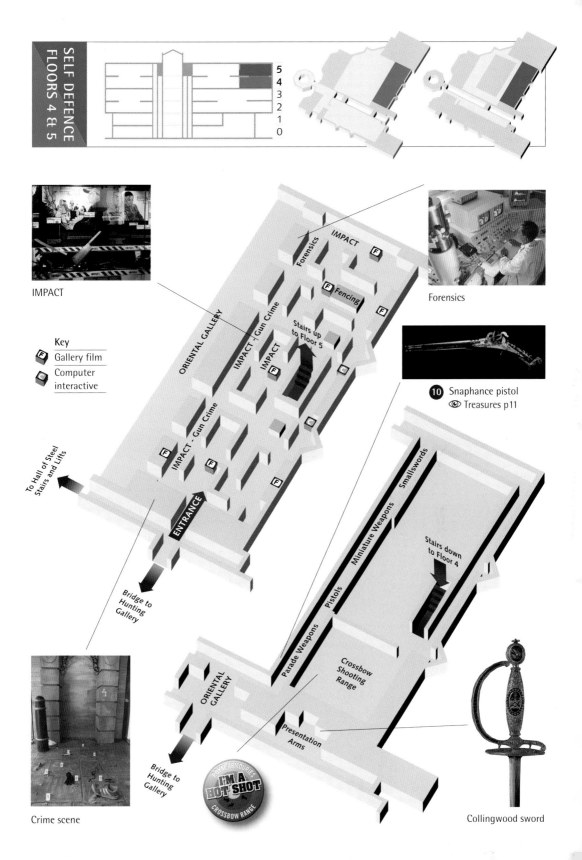

5
4
3
2
1
0

IMPACT

Forensics

Key

Ⓕ Gallery film

◆ Computer interactive

Forensics

IMPACT

ORIENTAL GALLERY

IMPACT - Gun Crime

IMPACT

Fencing

Stairs up to Floor 5

⑩ Snaphance pistol
👁 Treasures p11

To Hall of Steel Stairs and Lifts

IMPACT - Gun Crime

ENTRANCE

Smallswords

Miniature Weapons

Stairs down to Floor 4

Pistols

Parade Weapons

Bridge to Hunting Gallery

ORIENTAL GALLERY

Crossbow Shooting Range

Bridge to Hunting Gallery

ROYAL ARMOURIES
I'M A HOT SHOT
CROSSBOW RANGE

Presentation Arms

Crime scene

Collingwood sword

Self defence

In the Middle Ages very few people journeyed far from their homes. Roads in Britain and Europe were poor and there was a real danger of being attacked. With no organised police force to uphold the law, individuals had to protect themselves.

Buckler of wood reinforced by concentric steel rings attached by rivets. Welsh, about 1540. v.21

Scene from a film on show in the gallery.

Travellers, traders and pilgrims armed themselves with daggers, swords and quarterstaffs. Civilians did not usually wear armour, it was expensive and most people would not have been able to afford much more than a small shield (buckler). For those who could afford it, a coat of mail, worn under the tunic, would have offered extra protection.

Most classes in society openly carried swords and daggers as items of everyday dress. Although primitive handguns appeared in Europe before 1400, it was not until the early 16th century that a new firing mechanism and improved gunpowder made it possible to produce compact guns ready to fire at the pull of a trigger.

Handguns eventually became common enough to be a threat to civil order – especially the pistol which could be easily concealed.

The development of the flintlock by 1600 made the pistol a practical everyday weapon. By 1830 the flintlock had given way to the more reliable percussion lock, and by 1850 the single-shot weapon was often replaced by the multiple-shot revolver.

👁 Development of firearms pages 28-33

During the Victorian period crime was reduced, thanks to the increasingly effective police force, but fear of crime remained. It was common for law-abiding citizens to arm themselves with revolvers, pistols and knives. Some people carried more elegant concealed weapons such as the swordstick or the cane gun.

It was not until the 20th century that legal controls were introduced to limit the types of weapons which could be privately owned.

Scene from a film on show in the gallery.

Travel

Travelling the roads of England of the 17th and 18th century was a dangerous business as crime was rife. The growth of trade generated wealth and a travelling community. These traders and travellers represented rich pickings for the highwayman and footpad. There was no organised force to deter and detect crime. The country was served mostly by local constables and watch patrols who were often inefficient. In defence of their trade and profits, travellers armed themselves and their transport more heavily than before.

Smuggling
By 1750 smuggling had become big business. There was a growing demand for luxury goods such as tobacco, tea, brandy and silks brought from overseas. As these were subject to heavy import duties, large profits were to be made smuggling them into the country. Naturally the government was anxious to reduce this loss of customs and excise revenue and instructed the Coastguard, backed by the army and Royal Navy, to patrol the coastal waters and inland roads. The smugglers were often well armed and pitched battles between smugglers and 'revenue men' were not uncommon.

Travelling abroad
The coming of the industrial revolution in the 19th century and the invention of the railway and the steam train saw a rapid growth in the number of people travelling abroad. In this age of western imperialism more and more explorers, missionaries and hunters ventured out into uncharted regions across the globe.

Due the vast distances travelled much of the equipment needed had to be carried including not only the weapons for protection and hunting but also the means to repair them and to make ammunition. Small light engineering kits were developed incorporating extremely sophisticated and precise tools.

Stand and deliver!
Highwaymen thrived on the roads of England in the 17th and 18th century. Most were violent thugs but a few, such as Claude Duval, 'The Gallant Highwayman' (1643–70), who dressed fashionably, had impeccable manners and never used violence on his victims, had a certain flair and were regarded as romantic figures. To be robbed by a famous highwayman was considered something of an honour. Despite the inefficiency of the authorities most highwaymen ended up on the gallows at Tyburn – betrayed for blood money or by their own carelessness. Their bodies were hung in gibbets to rot as a warning to others.

Scene from a film on show in the gallery.

Civil forces

Public servants such as police and prison officers, Customs and Excise officers and Royal Mail coachmen were armed with a variety of weapons including edged weapons and firearms.

Mail coach guards

Poor roads made communication slow and difficult and post boys and coaches were often robbed. In 1784 a fast, well-protected nationwide system of coaches was set up. Every coach had a guard armed with a pair of flintlock pistols and a blunderbuss, which generally proved an effective defence.

The police

For many centuries law enforcement depended upon the local community. Magistrates appointed officers such as parish constables, who were unpaid, and watchmen to keep the peace.

In the 18th century, as towns expanded and population increased, this style of policing could not cope with the growing threats and fears of crime and disorder.

The first attempts at professional policing were made in London, and in 1829 the Metropolitan Police Force was established by Sir Robert Peel. It was not until 1856 that every local authority was required to have a police force.

With the Industrial Revolution and mass migration to the cities, law and order became increasingly important and a regular full-time paid force slowly developed.

The first police officers were armed with a wooden truncheon and sometimes a short sword. As firearms were increasingly used in crime the police were forced to respond by arming themselves and developing protective clothing.

A brass-barrelled flintlock blunderbuss, fitted with a spring-operated bayonet. English, about 1800. XII.1042

▶ British police equipment:

Police rattle, about 1840. XVIII.401

Metropolitan helmet for use on a moped, after 1952. IV.1826

Police truncheon, about 1950. XVIII.403

Police truncheon, painted with the monogram of King George IV, 1820–30. VIII.160

Fencing and duelling

Duelling was a way for 'gentlemen' to settle their quarrels. The duel of honour was fought in cold blood between gentlemen, one perhaps seeking 'satisfaction' from the other in response to an insult to his 'good name'.

An illustration from *The School of Fencing* – a manual by the famous fencing master, Henry Angelo, London, 1787.

Swords

At first personal combats were fought with a sword and a small shield (buckler).

The rapier, a longer, narrower and more pointed sword used for thrusting was introduced after 1500. It often had an elaborate guard to protect the unarmoured hand. A new style of fencing developed, emphasising the use of the point instead of the edge of the blade.

Swords were worn as part of a gentleman's everyday dress. One of the qualities thought to be desirable in a gentleman was his skill with a sword and there were many schools which taught the art of fencing. Although some students may have learned to use the sword with duelling in mind most considered it a sport. Schools of fencing, such as that in London of swordmaster Henry Angelo, became very popular.

Pistols

By about 1780 the pistol displaced the sword in the duel and many gentlemen owned a cased set of specialised duelling pistols. The duellist had to be able to aim and fire quickly and accurately, usually at a distance of not less than 15 m (50 feet).

Scene from a film on show in the gallery.

Two foil fencers in a French salon, wearing protective jackets and masks, about 1820.

The scene is a print of the 'famous' foil match between the Comte de Bordy and the fencing master Justin Lafaugère in 1816, after a watercolour c.1893 by Fréderic Régamey (1845-1925).

Making firearms

The manufacture of a firearm is more complex than making a sword. Different parts were manufactured by specialists and a whole army of craftsmen grew to satisfy growing military needs.

Barrels

The most important part of any firearm is the barrel – it has to withstand great pressure from the explosion and it has to be straight. Making barrels in the traditional way was probably the most demanding both of energy and skill of any branch of gunmaking.

Barrels were traditionally made from strips of iron coiled around a mandrel in stages to form a spiral tube (see below) and then the edges welded together by heating until white hot and hammering the joints, at the same time maintaining an equal thickness.

The barrel would then be bored out using a mechanically rotated tool to create an even, smooth bore, followed by polishing.

Locks and stocks

All the other parts of the gun had to be made by hand – each of the pieces which constituted the lock and trigger; the stock; the furniture; the ramrod; the bayonet; the bayonet scabbard. Most of these had their own specialists –

the lockplate filers, the springmakers and so on.

Being so labour intensive made guns quite expensive items of equipment because each stage in the making required a craftsman to be paid, on top of the costs of raw material. Also, because they were individually hand made, each part of a gun differed slightly from the same part in another gun, although they looked identical. This in itself created problems of repair on the battlefield. Parts from one scrap musket could not be used to repair another and get it back into action.

Patterns

This problem of interchangeability was first recognized by the French in the 18th century and they tried to devise a means of making each part so accurately that it would interchange with the same part on any gun. Honoré Le Blanc partly succeeded in 1777 by making locks in which each part could be interchanged, but the threat to traditional gunmakers caused riots and so the idea was dropped.

The idea was not lost however. It was taken to America by Thomas Jefferson. America suffered a drastic shortage of specialist craftsmen to make arms for the new country and the only way was to try to develop machines to do the work of craftsmen.

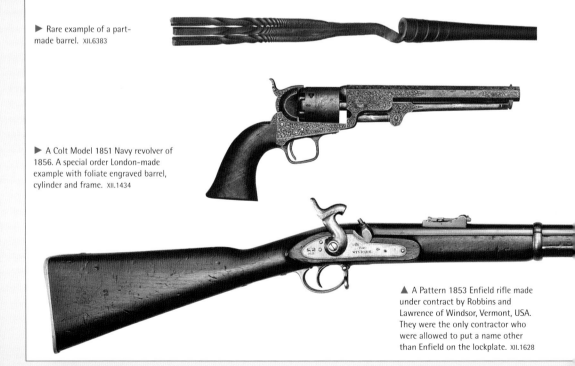

▶ Rare example of a part-made barrel. XII.6383

▶ A Colt Model 1851 Navy revolver of 1856. A special order London-made example with foliate engraved barrel, cylinder and frame. XII.1434

▲ A Pattern 1853 Enfield rifle made under contract by Robbins and Lawrence of Windsor, Vermont, USA. They were the only contractor who were allowed to put a name other than Enfield on the lockplate. XII.1628

Samuel Colt (1814–62)

Samuel Colt was a great supporter of this technology and did much to help it develop. By the late 1840s it had been brought to perfection, especially in the workshop of Robbins and Lawrence in the small town of Windsor, Vermont. Guns made by Robbins and Lawrence, each part being interchangeable, and by Colt, were exhibited at the Great Exhibition in 1851.

Colt set up a factory in London to cater for the sudden demand for his revolvers. Robbins and Lawrence were commissioned by the British Government to equip the new Royal Small Arms Manufactory at Enfield to make the new Pattern 1853 rifle.

Mass production

This new technology, relying on machines to do the specialised work and gauges to check finished sizes and ensure accuracy, was revolutionary in Europe which relied entirely on hand craftsmen. Costs were reduced and assembly was faster because each component no longer needed delicate adjustments by hand to be made to fit. In addition battlefield repair was simpler because the soldier could carry essential spares, such as springs, knowing that he could replace them easily. Also the government was no longer at the mercy of private contractors who could theoretically hold up production through strikes and virtually hold the country to ransom in times of war.

Craftsmanship

The old technology, however, continued in the private gun trade because each member of the gun-buying public wanted freedom to choose something which appealed to their tastes and needs. The hand-crafted gun became and still is the province of the sportsman.

This same technology which was developed to make guns was seen to have other possibilities too. It was adapted to make clocks and watches, sewing machines, typewriters, bicycles and eventually motor cars. It fathered the consumer society.

Engraving showing a power-driven automatic rifling machine of the type made by Robbins and Lawrence and supplied to Enfield.

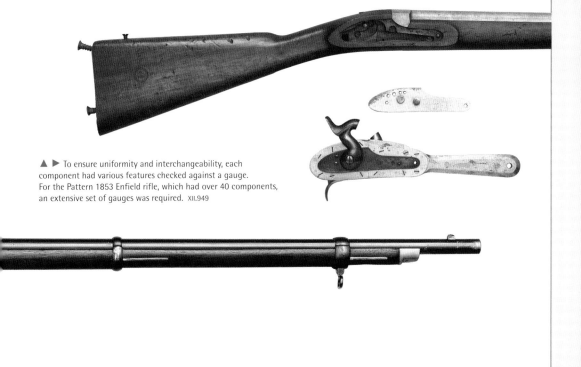

▲ ▶ To ensure uniformity and interchangeability, each component had various features checked against a gauge. For the Pattern 1853 Enfield rifle, which had over 40 components, an extensive set of gauges was required. XII.949

Development of swords

❶ Early swords

Between AD 300 and AD 900 a longer sword was developed. This had a two-edged blade and blunt tip and was designed for slashing and cutting at an opponent. These blades were often 'pattern-welded', that is made of steel and iron twisted and hammer-welded together, into the body of the blade. This allowed a more even distribution of strength. The blade was also fullered (*grooved*) to make it lighter and more flexible. The hilt was made up of a pommel, which balanced the weight of the blade, together with a simple cross-guard to protect the hand and the sword grip.

❷ ❸ Medieval

Swords were expensive possessions and throughout the Middle Ages the knight came to be identified by his sword. The typical knightly sword had a straight, centrally grooved blade designed for cutting and a simple cross guard. It symbolised wealth and power, as well as being a first-class fighting weapon.

As body armour developed the two-edged slashing blade became longer and had a stronger, more needle-like, point that could penetrate gaps in an opponent's plate armour. The sword-grip was also extended to allow it to be wielded with either one or two hands to enable the user to deliver more powerful blows.

In the 15th century two-handed swords were developed for fighting on foot. Finer control of the blade could be obtained by looping the forefinger over the guard (or quillons) and so, from the 14th century, a loop was sometimes added to protect the finger. During the 15th century knuckle-guards and further loops, constructed around the quillon, developed to protect the hand.

Pommel

Hilt

Guard or quillons

Blade

❸ Hand-and-a-half sword ◄
Probably Italian, about 1400-1410. IX.915

❷ Medieval sword ▼
European, 12th century. A typical knightly sword with a broad blade. IX.1082

❶ Early sword ►
Possibly Scandinavian, 900-1150. IX.859

❹ ❺ Renaissance

Renaissance Europe saw the development of the art of fencing and a greater emphasis on the use of the point emerged. Civilian swords, such as the rapier, had long, lighter blades and sharp points, designed primarily for thrusting, and developed complicated guards. The military broadsword retained its cutting edges and by the late 16th century, as the wearing of armour declined, the hand was also often enclosed in a combination of bars and plates to protect against the thrust.

Cavalry and infantry swords also tended to have basket hilts, the latter of less complex construction. Civilian swords however, not requiring robust construction became lighter, and shorter. The 'small sword' became a decorative, though still lethal, component of a gentleman's attire.

❻ ❼ Industrial Revolution

The Industrial Revolution in the West brought about the standardization of parts. From about 1700 many countries introduced regulation issue swords, such as the British patterns for the Heavy Cavalry sword and the Light Cavalry sword, both of 1796. Military swords often had hilts formed of brass or steel bars and cavalry swords had long curved blades designed for cutting. As the battlefield became increasingly dominated by firepower the sword declined, surviving only as a badge of military rank. Swords remained part of male civilian costume until the late 18th century but are now confined to either being presented by the State in gratitude to successful soldiers or public servants, or for ceremonial purposes and court duties only. (See page 80).

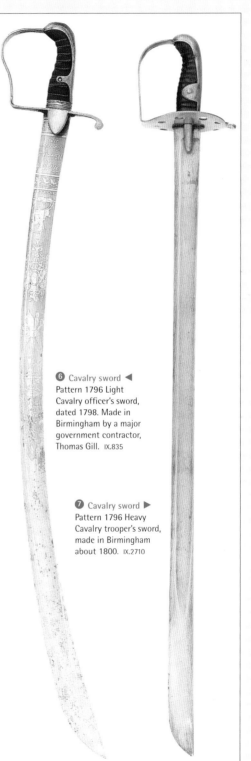

❻ Cavalry sword ◄
Pattern 1796 Light
Cavalry officer's sword,
dated 1798. Made in
Birmingham by a major
government contractor,
Thomas Gill. IX.835

❼ Cavalry sword ►
Pattern 1796 Heavy
Cavalry trooper's sword,
made in Birmingham
about 1800. IX.2710

❹ Rapier ▼
Italian, about 1600.
The whole hilt is
damascened in gold. XI.869

❺ Small sword ▼
French, Paris, about 1777. The
chiselled steel hilt is decorated
with four coloured gold. The
blade is blued and gilt. IX.936

◉ Decorating armour page 45

Making edged weapons

The skill of the edged weapon maker has been passed from generation to generation and as metals have developed so has the art of the sword maker.

Iron and steel

While only iron was available, sword and knife makers were at a disadvantage as it is soft and easily bent out of shape. It was discovered in antiquity that an alloy of iron and a small amount of carbon had the property of becoming hard when plunged red hot into water. However, this had the disadvantage that it also became brittle, but it was found that the brittleness could be overcome by reheating to a lower temperature and then cooling, a process known as tempering. This new type of iron was, in fact, steel.

Blades could now be made which held a good edge and were tough enough to withstand the rigours of use.

Pattern welding

This new steel was at first quite a rare and expensive commodity and to make best use of it, it was combined with soft iron in such a way that the steel formed the cutting edge while the soft iron formed the core of a blade. Sometimes the iron and steel were blended together and created a blade which had more uniform qualities. These blades, when etched, revealed a variety of swirling patterns and today are often referred to as pattern-welded blades.

Craftsmen

All of this required an extremely high degree of skill. There was no oxy-acetylene welding equipment or gas heating available. Everything had to be carried out using the forge's hearth in which the metal was heated, followed by welding the components together using the hammer on the anvil and then giving the blade its finished shape.

Polishing

Once the forging stage had been completed, the blade had to be ground and polished to give it a cutting edge and a fine finish, followed by etching to bring out the pattern if required. It then had to have some form of hilt fitted with which to hold the weapon.

Mechanisation

By the mid 19th century, the manufacture of military blades especially was beginning to be mechanized. Shaping of long blades was done by special rolling mills and shorter ones by forging hot steel in specially-shaped moulds, or dies. The role of the craftsmen in blade making was gradually being overtaken by the machine. But this was only true where large numbers of identical items were required, such as for military use.

Finishing touches

For special, one-off items the craftsman again came into his own especially in creating such things as elaborately decorated presentation swords requiring high degrees of manipulative and aesthetic skill.

👁 Decorating armour page 45

Sword and scabbard presented to Lt James Bowen by the Lloyd's Patriotic Fund, 1803, displaying a high degree of craftsmanship in the sculptural embellishment of the hilt and the blued and gilt inscription and decoration of the blade. IX.2565